THE CALEDONIAN STEAM PACKET COMPANY
An Illustrated History

Alistair Deayton

AMBERLEY

Front cover: Jeanie Deans seen from *Waverley*, June 1963.
Rear cover: Duchess of Montrose departing from Largs Pier in late summer 1963, her penultimate season.

First published 2014

Amberley Publishing
The Hill, Stroud
Gloucestershire, GL5 4EP

www.amberley-books.com

Copyright © Alistair Deayton, 2014

The right of Alistair Deayton to be identified as the Author of this work has been asserted in accordance with the Copyrights, Designs and Patents Act 1988.

ISBN 978 1 4456 3920 8 (print)
ISBN 978 1 4456 3931 4 (ebook)

British Library Cataloguing in Publication Data.
A catalogue record for this book is available from the British Library.

Typeset in 11pt on 12pt Sabon LT Std.
Typesetting by Amberley Publishing.
Printed in the UK.

CONTENTS

An Edwardian CSP official postcard, with views of Whiting Bay and Brodick.

INTRODUCTION

The Caledonian Steam Packet Company Limited (CSP) was founded in 1889 as a subsidiary of the Caledonian Railway to operate steamer services on the Clyde from that company's new terminal at Gourock and from Wemyss Bay. Various abortive efforts had been made to operate steamers by the railway companies from shortly after the opening of the Glasgow, Paisley & Greenock Railway in 1841, and again with the opening of the Wemyss Bay Railway in 1865, but the railway companies had decided to leave the operation of steamer services to the private operators, sometimes coming to an agreement with them to operate in connection with their trains.

The remaining two steamers of the late Captain Bob Campbell of Kilmun were purchased, and over the following decade a fleet of modern paddle steamers was built for the company. In 1890 services also commenced from Ardrossan (Montgomerie Pier) in connection with the newly opened Lanarkshire & Ayrshire Railway. The famous 'Teetotal Steamer' *Ivanhoe* was purchased in 1897 while 1906 saw the building of the company's first turbine steamer, *Duchess of Argyll*.

The First World War saw the entire fleet taken up by the Admiralty, mainly for minesweeping, with two steamers being lost to enemy action and another not being deemed worthy of refurbishment after the punishment it had received in war service. Meanwhile, the Clyde services were maintained by chartered tonnage. In 1922 a steamer on Loch Awe was taken over, as was the Loch Tay Steamboat Company Ltd.

The railway amalgamation of 1923 saw the Clyde services of the London, Midland & Scottish Railway continue to be operated by the CSP, which absorbed the steamers of the Glasgow & South Western Railway, and their services from Greenock (Princes Pier), Fairlie and Ardrossan (Winton Pier) were added. The 1930s saw a major building programme, with new paddle and turbine steamers entering service. In October 1935 the fleet of Williamson-Buchanan Steamers, almost the last surviving private operator on the Clyde, was taken over, although their steamers retained their own livery for a while.

The Second World War saw steamers again serving their country, again with losses and with some being too worn out for reconditioning after the end of the conflict. The Kyle of Lochalsh–Kyleakin car ferry service was taken over in 1945.

In 1948 the railways were nationalised, but the CSP continued as the operator of the railway steamers on the Clyde. The remaining steamers of the London & North Eastern Railway were absorbed in the fleet along with services from Craigendoran Pier, as well as the two surviving Loch Lomond steamers and the Loch Lomond steamer service. The early 1950s saw the first car ferries appear, as well as the building of a quartet of motor vessels, the Maids, and a new large paddle steamer for Loch Lomond. A larger car ferry for the Arran service, *Glen Sannox*, appeared in 1957.

On 1 January 1969 the CSP left railway control and became part of the Scottish Transport Group, which also owned the 50 per cent of David MacBrayne that had been held by British Railways and operated nationalised bus services in Scotland. Later in the same year, the company's first drive-through car ferry was purchased second-hand from a Swedish owner, and in the following year a sidewall hovercraft was introduced, which proved to be a short-lived experiment. On 31 December 1969 the Bute Ferry Company Ltd was purchased along with the short route across the Kyles of Bute from Colintraive to Rhubodach on Bute. The period from 1969 onwards saw some interchange of vessels between the CSP and MacBrayne. Later in 1969 the other 50 per cent of David MacBrayne had been purchased by the STG.

The CSP house flag was yellow with a lion rampant, a feature added to the funnels in 1965. However, from 1949 to 1951 inclusive, the BTC house flag was adopted for all ships; it was based on the former LNER house flag, but with the addition of the lion and wheel emblem, and was very similar to Waverley Steam Navigation's present-day house flag. The car ferry *Glen Sannox* had two magnificent features: the CSP crest on the bow, and a huge linoleum crest outside the bar and saloon. *Maid of the Loch* had the British Railways crest on her bow until 1970, when a demand from Gourock instructed that it be removed.

On 1 January 1973 the CSP and David MacBrayne Ltd were merged to form Caledonian MacBrayne Ltd, which continues to operate Clyde and West Highland ferry services to this day.

Chapter 1

BEFORE THE CSP: 1841–88

The Glasgow, Paisley & Greenock Railway opened from Glasgow's Bridge Street station to Greenock (Cathcart Street) on 30 March 1841. This was a short walk from Custom House Quay, although it meant passing through an insalubrious environment and many passengers were so frightened by this that they preferred to take the steamer direct from the Broomielaw in Glasgow rather than take the train to Greenock and connect with the steamer there.

Initially the railway company came to an agreement with various private owners to provide connecting services from Greenock to the Clyde coast towns, but in 1842 it formed the Railway Steam Packet Company, purchasing *Royal Victoria* (1838) to run to Helensburgh, and *Isle of Bute* (1835) and *Maid of Bute* (1835) to run to Dunoon and Rothesay. The first-named was sold in the following year and the others in 1846 and 1847 respectively.

In 1845 a trio of new steamers was built for the company, these being *Pilot*, *Petrel* and *Pioneer*. In 1846 all three were sold to G. & J. Burns, and the Railway Steam Packet Company ceased operations.

Pilot worked in the West Highlands and in 1850 was sold for service on Loch Lomond, where she sank on 17 July of that year after striking an uncharted rock, known to this day as the Pilot

Rock. She was raised and returned to service a month later, and left the loch when sold to Irish owners in 1853 for the Belfast–Bangor service, which she operated until scrapped in 1862.

Petrel was with Burns until around 1850 then came under the ownership of various Clyde operators, mainly being used as a 'Sunday Breaker' until she was broken up in 1885. She also had a spell on the Belfast–Bangor service, from 1860 to 1864.

Pioneer had a long career in the West Highlands for Burns, Hutcheson and MacBrayne, remaining in service until 1893. She was on the Glasgow–Ardrishaig service until replaced by *Mountaineer* in 1852, and then operated out of Oban. She was re-boilered and rebuilt with a clipper bow in 1862, and lengthened in the winter of 1874/5, when a second funnel was added.

In 1851 the Glasgow, Paisley & Greenock Railway was taken over by the Caledonian Railway, and in 1852 the new Railway Steamboat Company was formed and three small steamers were built for them, *Gourock*, *Helensburgh* and *Dunoon*, operating from Glasgow to Greenock, from Greenock to Helensburgh and the Gareloch, and to Dunoon and the Holy Loch respectively. Towards the end of 1852 *Helensburgh* and *Dunoon* were sold for use in Australia in connection with a gold rush there. The former operated there until she was wrecked in 1859, but the latter sank in the Bay of Biscay on her delivery voyage. *Gourock* was sold abroad in 1853 and by 1861 was operating at Riga, Latvia, where she was still active as late as 1906.

The Railway Steamboat Company purchased four steamers in 1853, *Glasgow Citizen*, *Eva*, *Lochlomond* and *Flamingo*. At the end of the summer of 1853 the company was wound up and arrangements made with the private owners for rail-connected services.

Glasgow Citizen had been built in 1852 for J. Barr, and was sold to Australia in 1854, where she operated from Melbourne to Geelong until she was sold for use in the New Zealand Gold Rush in 1861, being wrecked on her delivery voyage there in October of the following year.

Eva was new in 1853 and was sold to Australian owners in December of that year; she sank off Lambey Island on her delivery voyage on 27 December of the same year.

Lochlomond had been built in 1845 for the Dumbarton Steamboat Co.'s Glasgow–Dumbarton service. She was sold to Mersey owners in 1854 and worked there for a further ten years.

Flamingo was new in 1853 and was also sold to Australia but sank in the mid-Atlantic on her delivery voyage under the name *Bell Bird*.

It should be said that all the steamers that sailed for Australia in that era made the journey out under sail, with the engines packed as cargo and reinstalled after arrival in the Antipodes.

In 1865 the Greenock & Wemyss Bay Railway Company opened its line from Port Glasgow to a new pier at Wemyss Bay. They had formed the Wemyss Bay Steamboat Company in the previous year to operate steamer services from Wemyss Bay. Two large steamers were ordered from Caird's yard in Greenock for the service, but one was sold on the stocks for blockade-running in the American Civil War. She was named *Hattie* and was lost on 8 May 1865 en route from Cork to Nassau, never having the opportunity to run the blockade. The two others were named *Kyles* and *Bute*, and entered service on 15 May and at the end of June 1865. They were joined by the smaller *Largs*, which had started sailing in April 1865, initially from Glasgow to Millport before the railway was opened to Wemyss Bay on 15 May. *Victory*, which had been built in 1864 for the Glasgow–Rothesay service, was purchased at the end of June. *Kyles* and *Bute* were too large for the traffic offered, and were sold in 1866 to Thames owners, becoming *Albert Edward* and *Princess Alice* respectively; the latter sank in 1878 with the loss of around 800 lives, the worst disaster in British pleasure steamer history. *Albert Edward* remained in service on the Thames until she was scrapped in 1889. *Largs* and *Victory* continued in service for the company and were joined in April 1866 by *Argyle*, which had been built earlier in that year for the Glasgow–Rothesay route. In January 1869 the railway company ceased steamer-owning and came to an agreement with Gillies & Campbell to operate the rail-connected services from Wemyss Bay. The railway company was taken over by the Caledonian Railway in 1893, although the train services had always been worked by the latter company.

Largs was sold to Ireland for use in the Shannon Estuary, where she served from Limerick to Foynes and Kilrush until she was scrapped in 1903; *Victory* had a peripatetic career under various Clyde owners, most notably as *Cumbrae* for Hill & Co., until sold for use as a coal hulk at Newry in 1897; while *Argyle* went to Dundee owners in 1890 for service on the Tay and was sold to Spain in 1904, being broken up four years later.

Left: Lochlomond of 1845, seen passing Dumbarton Rock. She ran for the Railway Steam Packet Co. from 1852 until 1854.

Right: Pioneer, late in her long career, berthed at Corpach.

Above left: *Petrel* of 1844 in her original condition.

Above right: The Wemyss Bay Steamship Company's *Bute* of 1865.

Left: The Wemyss Bay Steamship Company's *Largs*, lying bow out across the end of Rothesay Pier, with Hutcheson's *Iona* of 1864 at the pier face behind her.

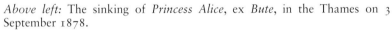

Above left: The sinking of *Princess Alice*, ex *Bute*, in the Thames on 3 September 1878.

Above right: *Victory* in later life as Hill & Co.'s *Cumbrae* on the Fairlie–Cumbrae service between 1982 and 1991.

Right: *Victory*, of the Wemyss Bay Steamship Company, from an illustration in the Wotherspoon Collection at the Mitchell Library.

Argyle lying across the east end of Rothesay Pier, showing the pier almost exactly like it is today, with the exception of the linkspan.

Chapter 2

THE CALEDONIAN RAILWAY ERA: 1889–1922

On 6 January 1889 the Caledonian Railway opened an extension from Greenock (Central), via the Newton Street Tunnel underneath Greenock, to a magnificent new pier at Gourock. They formed the Caledonian Steam Packet Company Ltd to operate steamer services on the Firth of Clyde, and these commenced operating from Gourock on 1 June 1889.

In December 1888 *Meg Merrilies* and *Madge Wildfire*, the two remaining steamers of the late Captain Bob Campbell's fleet of Kilmun steamers, were purchased by the Caledonian Railway, and they were transferred to the new company on 5 May 1889. Captain Bob had died in April 1888 and his two sons, Peter and Alex, had decamped along with the 1885 *Waverley* to the Bristol Channel, where, as P. & A. Campbell, they would found the major excursion shipping company in that area, a company that would continue in operation until early 1981.

Meg Merrilies had been built in 1883 for the North British Steam Packet Co., but had been rejected by them as being too slow. She was chartered for the Belfast–Bangor trade in 1884 and purchased by Captain Campbell in 1885. She was re-boilered in the winter of 1887/88, when she was reduced from two funnels to one, and new boilers were again fitted in 1893 and 1898. The 1898 boilers were experimental Haythorn ones, but after an explosion in the boiler room in January 1900, she was again re-boilered with conventional boilers. She was mainly used on the service from Gourock to the Holy Loch, and was sold in July 1902 to the Leopoldina Railway in Brazil and renamed *Maua*. A wooden turtle deck was built over the exposed foredeck for her delivery voyage to Brazil. She operated in Rio do Janeiro harbour and ended her days when she was broken up there in 1921.

Madge Wildfire had been built in 1886 for the through Glasgow–Kilmun service, on which she continued to operate until 1908, being used after that on the route from Gourock to the Holy Loch. She received new boilers and compound engines in 1891. She was sold in 1911 to Captain Cameron of Dumbarton for excursion services, and in 1913 went to Buchanan Steamers Ltd as *Isle of Skye*. The year 1927 saw a sale to the Grangemouth & Forth Towing Co. for service on the Firth of Forth out of Leith as *Fair Maid*. During the Second World War she was used as a decontamination vessel at Greenock, and in 1944 she saw service on the Firth again when she replaced *Lucy Ashton* on the Craigendoran–Dunoon service for ten days, and also spent one day on the Gourock–Kilmun service. By the end of the war she was worn out and was scrapped in 1946.

The first steamer built for the CSP was *Caledonia*, which was delivered from her builders in June 1889. She was of a design that by then had become standard for a Clyde paddle steamer, with an open foredeck, fore and after deck saloons extending to the edge of the hull, and a promenade deck above these. Her machinery was of an innovative design, a tandem compound engine with two cylinders on one crank. In 1893 she was experimentally converted from coal to oil firing, but reverted to coal firing in the spring of the following year after an increase in the price of oil. A brief spell of oil firing was again tried in 1897. In 1903 her bridge was moved forward of the funnel. She was initially operated from Gourock to Dunoon and Rothesay, and from May 1890 was on the Wemyss Bay–Millport service, but after the sale of *Meg Merrilies* in 1902 she moved to the Holy Loch service, which she maintained for the remainder of her career. She served as a minesweeper from April 1917 until April 1919 and was withdrawn and sold for scrapping at the end of 1933. Her paddle box crest, along with a selection of photographs, was on display at Gourock station until the 1970s.

Galatea was a larger two-funnelled steamer which entered service in July 1889, sailing from Gourock to Rothesay, with an afternoon cruise round Bute. She had conventional two-crank compound machinery, which was felt to be too powerful for the hull, leading to her inability to reach her top design speed. In 1890 she was moved to longer excursion services from Wemyss Bay, in 1891 to a service from Rothesay to Arrochar, and in 1893 was back on the round Bute cruises. In 1903 she was used as a reserve steamer, and in 1906 was sold to Italian owners for a service from Genoa to Nice. In 1914 she was broken up at Palermo, Sicily.

The year 1890 saw the arrival of the sister ships *Marchioness of Breadalbane* and *Marchioness of Bute*, both very similar to *Caledonia* with tandem compound machinery, but the bridge forward of the funnel. Both operated on the services out of Wemyss Bay, to Rothesay and to Millport respectively. The former was used as a minesweeper from April 1917 until 1 May 1919 under the name HMS *Marquis of Breadalbane* and returned to Clyde service after the war, being transferred to the Holy Loch run after the demise of *Caledonia* in 1933 until sold for scrapping in 1935. She was purchased from the scrapyard and used for excursion work from Great Yarmouth and Lowestoft, and also briefly from Newcastle, until she was sold to German shipbreakers in April 1937.

Marchioness of Bute was sold in July 1908 for use on the River Tay, and was used as a minesweeper during the First World War, but was laid up at Inverkeithing after that until she was broken up in 1923.

In September 1888 the Lanarkshire & Ayrshire Railway was opened from Barrmill to Ardrossan (Montgomerie Pier), although the line from Cathcart to Giffen Junction via Neilston, Uplawmoor and Lugton did not open until 1 May 1903, and in 1890 the CSP commenced operating from Ardrossan to the Arran piers of Brodick, Lamlash and Whiting Bay. A large, powerful new steamer, *Duchess of Hamilton*, was built for this service. She was the first Clyde steamer to have the promenade deck extended to the bow, although the main deck below this was open at the sides for rope handling. With a length of 250 feet, she was 50 feet longer than the Marchionesses and 20 feet longer than *Galatea*. She had two-crank compound machinery and her passenger accommodation was magnificently fitted out. In 1906, with the advent of *Duchess of Argyll*, she was moved to operate excursions from Gourock. In February 1915 she was taken over by the Admiralty and converted to a minesweeper. On 29 November 1915 she struck a mine and sank off Harwich.

Marchioness of Lorne entered service in 1891. She was of a similar size to the other Marchionesses but had her promenade deck extended to the bow and had unusual tandem triple-expansion machinery with four cylinders, two on each of the two cranks, one with a high-pressure and an intermediate-pressure cylinder and one with a second high-pressure and a low-pressure cylinder. She was used on the Arran service in winter and on rail-connected services from Wemyss Bay in the summer. In 1909 she moved to the Wemyss Bay–Millport service. She served her country as a minesweeper from 1916 onwards, based at Malta and Port Said. On her return from war service she was laid up until scrapped in 1923.

It may be of interest here to give some detail of the colour scheme of the CSP steamers before 1914. Cameron Somerville, in his booklet *Colour on the Clyde*, gives a very detailed description of what, in black-and-white photographs, appears to be a very basic livery:

> The Caledonian Steam Packet Co. had an attractive colour scheme of green underbody (this was experimental and was later changed to the brown which remained until the end), white boot-topping, giving to a blue-black hull with two gold lines. The exterior decoration of the saloons was intricate but lovely, giving indeed some colour on the Clyde. Commencing downwards from the 6-inch skirting-board at the rail of the promenade deck, there came first a narrow band of pale blue, then all the saloon was pink down to the window framing. (Each window – the glass – in these days was always set in a rolled frame and never in an opening, nakedly cut or punched out of a steel sheet.) The framework of each window was painted in white enamel with a beading of pale blue down the vertical edges. The astragals, or the very narrow uprights between the frames, were then of the main colour – pale pink with a vertical white bar down the middle. The glass of each window was divided vertically down the centre by teak, but the uppermost 1/6th or 1/4th was of little vertical panes of coloured glass, these forming one piece which opened inwards and downwards as a fanlight. Of course the scheme differed from steamer to steamer as there were only three sister ships in the Caley fleet. The windows of all the Clyde boats were large and many, amazingly so, considering the stormy passages that had so often to be made. The dazzling white paddle boxes carried the glorious badge of her name, with the name itself in gold leaf on a pale blue ground. The yellow funnel was done in columite, which, of course, you all know.

The next, and arguably the finest, paddle steamer to appear, in 1895, was *Duchess of Rothesay*. She was a smaller edition of *Duchess of Hamilton*, with two-crank compound machinery, and was 25 feet shorter than the latter. She entered service from Gourock and Wemyss Bay to Rothesay. Prior to 1914 she was known as the 'cock of the walk' and had a small weathercock at the top of her mast. In 1897 she took over *Ivanhoe*'s service from Gourock to Arran via the Kyles of Bute, and in the peak summer seasons of 1911 and 1914 was on the Ardrossan–Arran service. She was used as a minesweeper from October 1915, bearing the name HMS *Duke of Rothesay* from 1917 until 1919. On 1 June 1919 she sank at her moorings at Merklands Wharf when her ropes were tied tight at high tide, and she canted over as the tide fell, filled with water, broke her mooring ropes and settled on the riverbed. She was raised on 28 July and returned to Clyde service on 29 March 1920, operating from then until 1939 from Greenock (Princes Pier) and Gourock to Rothesay and the Kyles of Bute. She served as a minesweeper again from October 1939 until April 1942, under her own name, and was then an accommodation ship at Brightlingsea. Following war service she was sold for scrapping in the Netherlands.

Ivanhoe, a large two-funnelled steamer which had been built in 1880 as a teetotal steamer for the Frith (sic) of Clyde Steam Packet Co. Ltd, was purchased by the CSP in 1897. She had operated from Craigendoran, Greenock (Princes Pier) and Gourock to Arran via the Kyles of Bute for most of her career apart from a spell in spring 1894 when she had been chartered to operate cruises on the then newly opened Manchester Ship Canal. The first thing that the CSP did when they purchased her was to install a bar aboard. She was mainly used for excursions from Gourock for the CSP: on Mondays to Arrochar, Tuesdays and Thursdays to Millport, continuing on Tuesdays round Arran and on Thursdays round Ailsa Craig, on Wednesdays and Fridays round the lochs, and sailing as a general relief steamer on Saturdays. In 1911 she was sold to the Firth of Clyde Steam Packet Ltd, operating from Glasgow to Rothesay, and was sold again in June 1914 to Turbine Steamers Ltd, for whom she ran from Glasgow to Lochgoilhead as a replacement for *Edinburgh Castle*, which had been broken up in the previous year. Laid up on the outbreak of war, she was chartered to the CSP between 1916 and 1919 and was broken up in September 1919.

In 1902 *Duchess of Montrose* was built. She was 15 feet shorter than *Duchess of Rothesay* and had tandem triple expansion machinery, like *Marchioness of Lorne*. She was instantly recognisable by her very small paddle boxes. In her first season she offered excursions from Ayr, but was then used for general rail-connected work in the upper Firth. In February 1915 she was used as a troop transport from Southampton to France, and from May 1915 was requisitioned by the Admiralty and converted to a minesweeper, bearing, according to some sources, the name HMS *Montrose*. On 18 March 1917 she was lost after striking a mine near Gravelines, near Dunkirk, with the loss of life of twelve crew members.

The year 1903 saw a quasi-sister ship to *Duchess of Montrose* appear in the form of *Duchess of Fife*. She had similar machinery and was on the Gourock–Dunoon and Rothesay service for most of her career. She served from May 1916 to April 1919 as the minesweeper HMS *Duchess*, and again from 1939 to 1945 as a minesweeper, this time under her own name. She was present at the Dunkirk evacuation in 1940, and rescued 1,633 men on three trips back to Ramsgate. From 1937 she was on the route from Wemyss Bay to Millport and Kilchattan Bay and made her final sailing on 6 June 1953, by which time she was the final pre-First World War steamer in service on the Firth of Clyde for the CSP. She was sold for scrapping on 12 September of that year.

The turbine steamer had been introduced to the Clyde by *King Edward* in 1901, and in 1906 the CSP introduced their first turbine, *Duchess of Argyll*. Built by Denny at Dumbarton, she was initially open-decked forwards on the main deck like the CSP paddle steamers, but in March 1910 this area was plated in. Her forward windows on the main deck saloon were replaced by portholes at the same time. This was to make her suitable for winter refit work on the Stranraer–Larne service. She was initially on the Ardrossan–Arran run but was laid up in 1909 following the agreement between the CSP and the

GSWR (see below) and from then onwards was available for relief work on the Stranraer–Larne service, although the only spell she had on that was from 12 to 17 June 1911. The years 1910, 1912 and 1914 were spent on the Arran service, and in 1911 and 1913 she served on the Arran via the Kyles run. From February 1915 to April 1919 she served as a troop transport on the English Channel. She crossed the Channel 655 times between February 1915 and April 1919, carrying 326,608 men and steaming 71,624 miles. In September 1915 she went to the aid of the Williamson paddle steamer *Queen-Empress*, which had been in a collision with a destroyer, and towed her into Boulogne. In 1918, she escorted the Great Eastern Railway's *Archangel* (1910), also in use as a troop transport, back to port after she had also been in a collision with a destroyer. Her services were from Southampton, Weymouth and Dover to Rouen, Le Havre, Boulogne and Calais. In 1920 she returned to the Arran via the Kyles service, which she maintained until 1935. In 1936, following the absorption of the Turbine Steamers and Williamson-Buchanan Steamers fleets into the CSP, she sailed to Inveraray and Campbeltown three days a week to each destination. During the Second World War she remained in Clyde service, operating from Gourock to Dunoon and as a tender to troopships moored at the Tail of the Bank. Post-war she was on the Princes Pier and Gourock–Kyles of Bute service and was sold in February 1952 to the Admiralty for use, after her engines had been removed, as a floating laboratory at Portland, a job which she had until Easter 1969, being scrapped in the following year at Newhaven.

In 1908 the intense competition between the CSP and the Glasgow & South Western Railway, particularly on the Arran service, was proving financially ruinous, and an agreement to co-operate was made; steamers of each company would be laid up in alternate years and competing sailings would be combined.

During the First World War the entire CSP fleet was requisitioned by the Admiralty, and essential services on the Clyde were maintained by chartered tonnage. In addition to *Ivanhoe* (see above), *Iona*, *Chevalier* and *Fusilier* were chartered from David MacBrayne Ltd, and *Benmore* from John Williamson & Co. Most received the CSP yellow funnel, apart from *Chevalier* and *Iona*, which retained the red and black MacBrayne funnel, although *Iona* spent a short spell with the CSP yellow.

In 1922 four inland loch screw steamers were taken over by the CSP. *Countess of Breadalbane*, built in 1882 for service on Loch Awe, was taken over from the Lochawe Hotel Co. Ltd. She remained in service until she was broken up in 1936. At the time of her purchase, she had been laid up since 1914. She operated from Lochawe Pier to Ford at the south end of the loch.

The Loch Tay Steamboat Company Ltd was taken over with three operating screw steamers, *Lady of the Lake* (1882), cargo steamer *Sybilla* (1882), both of which were broken up in 1929, and twin screw steamer *Queen of the Lake* (1907), which operated until 1939 and on the outbreak of war was laid up on the slipway at Kenmore until she was sold for breaking up in 1950. A further cargo steamer, *Carlotta*, was taken over but saw little or no service under the CSP flag and was broken up in 1923. The service was twice daily from Loch Tay Pier at Killin along the lake to Kenmore, with a number of intermediate calls along the way. The pier at Killin was reached by rail, on an extension of the Killin branch line, and Kenmore Pier was served by bus from Aberfeldy.

Above left: Gourock Pier in a view from a postcard posted in 1905. Note the large 'Caledonian Railway' sign above the pier. It was changed to 'LMSR' and then to 'BR' and lasted until recent years, when that part of the pier was demolished. MacBrayne's *Columba* is seen arriving at the pier.

Above right: Madge Wildfire at the Broomielaw on the Glasgow–Kilmun service, with *Clutha No. 4* passing her bow.

Left: Meg Merrilies between 1889 and 1902 in CSP colours.

Opposite page: Madge Wildfire in old age as *Fair Maid*, moored at Craigendoran on VE Day, 8 May 1945.

Caledonia off Kirn on 9 September 1933, two months prior to her withdrawal from service.

Left: Galatea, one-time flagship of the CSP fleet.

Opposite page: Galatea with a full crowd of passengers aboard.

Marchioness of Breadalbane in post-1925 colours, with her fore saloon windows and sponsons covered over by winter boarding.

Above left: Marchioness of Bute; note the more vertical funnel, which distinguished her from her sister.

Above right: Duchess of Hamilton on a colour postcard, posted in 1908.

Right: Duchess of Hamilton bites into a storm off Ardrossan. A large copy of this was on display in the dining saloon of the 1932 turbine *Duchess of Hamilton* in the 1960s.

Marchioness of Lorne in Lamlash Bay.

Marchioness of Lorne, winter-boarded fore and aft, on the Arran service.

Duchess of Rothesay arriving at Dunoon in her 1925–39 condition.

Above left: Ivanhoe in 1894, while still owned by Captain James Williamson.

Above right: Ivanhoe at speed on the Firth in the colours of the Firth of Clyde Steam Packet Co. Ltd between 1911 and 1914.

Left: Ivanhoe at Arrochar, lying outside the GSWR's *Minerva* and the NB's *Lady Rowena*.

Opposite page: Duchess of Montrose off Holy Isle. Note the very small paddle boxes, which were her distinguishing feature.

Duchess of Fife berthed at Wemyss Bay before 1914. Note the coal wagons on the low-level track on the pier forward of the steamer, and the throngs of passengers both on the steamer and on the pier, about to board.

Duchess of Fife in 1952, after a wheelhouse had been added, in Rothesay Bay.

Above left: *Duchess of Fife* berthed at Rothesay in the twilight of her career in the early 1950s.

Above right: *Duchess of Argyll* at Brodick between 1910 and 1914, with a flotilla of torpedo boats moored in the bay.

Left: *Duchess of Argyll* in her early condition with open sides on the main deck at the bow, and large windows in the forward saloon, both of which were replaced by portholes in March 1910 for possible use on the Stranraer–Larne run.

Above left: Countess of Breadalbane at Ford Pier in her 1923–4 'tartan lum' colours.

Above right: Duchess of Argyll post-1948, with a wheelhouse installed.

Right: A promotional card of the Loch Awe steamer *Countess of Breadalbane.*

CHEAP DAY TRIPS FROM ALL CALEDONIAN RAILWAY STATIONS.

LUNCH, TEA, ETC., SERVED ON BOARD.

DUNCAN FRASER PROPRIETOR.

SALOON STEAMER "COUNTESS OF BREADALBANE" ON LOCHAWE.

Above left: Lady of the Lake on Loch Tay in an Edwardian postcard view posted in 1904.

Above right: Loch Tay steamer *Queen of the Lake* of 1907.

Left: Lady of the Lake at Kenmore Pier with the cargo steamer *Sybilla* in the foreground.

Chapter 3

THE LMS ERA: 1923–47

On 1 January 1923 the railway companies in Great Britain were amalgamated to form four large companies. Both the Caledonian and the Glasgow & South Western railways became part of the London Midland & Scottish Railway. The Clyde steamer services continued under the CSP umbrella with the addition of the GSWR steamers. Services from Greenock (Princes Pier), Fairlie and Ardrossan (Winton Pier), along with the excursion programme from Ayr, were now operated by the CSP, although the steamers were owned by the LMSR and not the CSP. The last survivor, *Glen Rosa*, was transferred to CSP ownership in her penultimate year, 1938.

Initially, the livery of the two companies was combined in what was called the 'tartan lum', with a yellow funnel with black top and a red band below the black top. In 1923 the GSWR steamers retained their grey hulls, but 1924 saw black hulls throughout the fleet and a narrower red band on the former GSWR steamers, and in 1925 the red band was removed and the colour scheme that would remain until 1964 was installed.

The GSWR steamers still around in 1923 were *Glen Sannox*, *Mercury*, *Glen Rosa*, *Jupiter*, *Juno*, the turbine *Atalanta*, the paddle tugs *Troon* and *Ayr* and the dredger *Kyle*. *Neptune* and

Mars had been lost during the war and *Minerva* sold at the end of the war when in Turkish waters.

Glen Sannox had been built in 1892 for the Ardrossan–Arran service to compete with *Duchess of Hamilton*, and was 10½ feet longer and slightly faster. She was the fastest ever Clyde paddle steamer, making over 20 knots on trials. She had two funnels, her promenade deck was extended to the bow and the main deck below that was plated in. She had been laid up in 1910 and operated to Arran via the Kyles in 1912. She had seen very brief war service in early 1915 as a troopship from Southampton to Le Havre but was returned to her owners after only one trip after she was unable to cope with heavy weather. She had returned to the Ardrossan–Arran route after the war, and was withdrawn at the end of the 1924 season and broken up in May 1925. Her early demise was due to her prodigious thirst for coal and hence high operating costs.

Mercury, also from 1892, was a conventional paddle steamer with an open foredeck and two-cylinder compound engines. She had operated from Greenock (Princes Pier) to Rothesay and the Kyles of Bute, but under the LMS she was on rail-connected services from Greenock (Princes Pier),

Gourock and Wemyss Bay until she was withdrawn after the 1933 season and sold for breaking up.

Glen Rosa had been built in 1893, along with sister ship *Minerva*, and operated from Fairlie to Millport, Kilchattan Bay and Rothesay until 1937, when she was used for special excursions and as a spare steamer. She was laid up in 1939 and sold for breaking up a month before war broke out in September of that year.

Jupiter was a larger steamer, built in 1896 with her promenade deck extended to the bow. Prior to 1914 she had been on the Arran via the Kyles service, and post-war she ran from Greenock to Ayr and on a variety of excursion sailings from the upper Firth. In 1931 she operated from Rothesay to Millport and to Loch Long, and in 1935 on the Fairlie–Millport and Rothesay roster. She was sold for scrapping in December 1936.

Juno had been purchased on the stocks in 1898 after the Thames company, which had ordered her, had gone out of business. She was larger and more sturdily built than the remainder of the GSWR fleet, apart from *Glen Sannox*, which was 15 feet longer. She was used on the excursion sailings out of Ayr and continued in this trade until she was withdrawn after the 1931 season. She was scrapped in the following year.

Atalanta had been the only turbine steamer built for the GSWR, in 1906. She was smaller than the other Clyde turbines, only having a single funnel, and had been built for the Ardrossan–Arran service, and moved to the Wemyss Bay–Millport station in 1936 after the introduction of *Marchioness of Graham*. She was sold in 1937 for use out of Blackpool, and was on a Fleetwood–Barrow service. She served in the Second World War as a net inspection and boom defence vessel and ended the war laid up at Methil, from where she was sold for scrapping in Belgium in 1946.

The paddle tugs *Troon* (1902) and *Ayr* (1897) and the steam bucket dredger *Kyle* (1885) were also taken over from the GSWR, and served until 1930, 1930 and 1950 respectively.

The first vessel built for the CSP after the grouping was the turbine steamer *Glen Sannox* in 1925. She was an almost exact copy of *Duchess of Argyll*, built nineteen years previously. She can be distinguished from her in photographs by having two ferry doors on her main deck, compared to one on the older vessel, and by the narrow black tops to her funnels. It was originally intended that she be named *Duchess of Atholl*. She was on the Ardrossan–Arran service and also gave evening cruises on occasion, and Sunday cruises from Ayr in the late 1920s. From 1936 to 1939 her Arran service was extended to Campbeltown. She was on the Stranraer–Larne service from 6 to 9 September 1939, just after the outbreak of war, and continued on the Arran service throughout the war years, sailing from Fairlie rather than Ardrossan. Services resumed from Ardrossan on 6 May 1946. *Glen Sannox* was withdrawn on 30 September 1953 and was sold for breaking up at Ghent in July of the following year.

The paddle tug *Walney* (1904) was transferred from Barrow to Troon, and from the LMSR to the CSP in 1930 to replace *Troon*. She served there until 1950. She had also carried passengers when at Barrow, but the passenger accommodation was not used during her spell in Scottish waters.

The year 1930 saw the building of the turbine steamer *Duchess of Montrose* for excursion service from the upper Firth. She was much more modern than *Glen Sannox*, and had an enclosed promenade deck with an observation lounge forwards with Lloyd Loom chairs. She was mainly used on the long-distance excursions from Gourock including Stranraer (to 1935), Round Arran and Ailsa Craig, and Round the Lochs. From 1936 she added a weekly trip to Inveraray. She remained on the Clyde during the war on the Wemyss Bay–Rothesay route and sailed to Arran via the Kyles in 1946. From 1947 to 1964 she sailed to Inveraray twice a week, made a Saturday afternoon cruise round Ailsa Craig, ran Sunday afternoon cruises alternately to Lochranza Bay and Cataciol and to the Arran Coast and round Holy Isle, and took her turn on the Campbeltown service. Originally she had a short half-height mainmast, but a full-height one was fitted in 1934. In 1948 a wheelhouse was fitted, as with the other CSP steamers, reportedly at the urging of the National Union of Railwaymen, and in 1956 she was converted to oil-firing. *Duchess of Montrose* was withdrawn from service after the 1964 season, and was sold for scrapping in Belgium in the following August.

In 1932 a sister ship, *Duchess of Hamilton*, appeared, although she was built by Harland & Wolff at their Govan yard rather than Denny. She had a full-height mainmast from the beginning and could be distinguished from her sister by having a crosstrees on the mainmast from 1939 onwards, four windows rather than three forward of the engine room grating on the main deck and two decks below the area between the funnels. She was placed on excursions from Ayr as a replacement for *Juno*. She was used as a troop transport from Stranraer to Larne between 1939 and 1945, and was mainly on the Campbeltown run from 1946 onwards, also sailing to Arran via the Kyles once weekly, and to Ayr via Brodick once weekly. The Sunday sailing to Campbeltown called at Lochranza outbound and at Brodick on the return journey from 1961 onwards. She exchanged rosters with *Duchess of Montrose* from time to time. She was converted to oil-firing in 1956. From 1965 onwards, following the withdrawal of her sister, the two turbine rosters were

combined, with Inveraray cut to once a week and Campbeltown to thrice weekly. She was withdrawn after the 1970 season and was sold in the following year for proposed use as a restaurant in Glasgow. Her after promenade deck was enclosed, but planning regulations put paid to the idea. She was sold again to hotelier and restaurateur Reo Stakis, but remained laid up in the East India Harbour in Greenock until she was sold for scrapping at Troon in April 1974.

The year 1934 saw the arrival of a pair of unconventional-looking paddle steamers, *Mercury* and *Caledonia*. Both had disguised paddle boxes with no vents, supposedly to make them look like a turbine steamer. This look was in line with the streamlined styles of the 1930s. Both had an upper deck above the aft deck saloon, extended forward to a viewing area below the bridge. The link between these two areas was by a hinged walkway on either side. This could be raised when high vehicles were carried. The area between the funnels was used for the carriage of cars in the correct tidal conditions. They were not true sister ships, though, *Mercury* coming from the Fairfield yard and *Caledonia* from Denny at Dumbarton. Both had triple expansion machinery.

Mercury was initially on the Greenock (Princes Pier) and Gourock to Rothesay service, and was switched to operate excursions from Rothesay in 1936, and the Arran via the Kyles run in 1939. In September 1939 she was requisitioned by the Admiralty and converted to a minesweeper, being based at Milford Haven, and on Christmas Eve 1940 she sank under tow after her stern was blown off by a mine off the Irish Coast.

Caledonia was on the Wemyss Bay–Rothesay and Millport service initially, also being used on afternoon excursions, and from 1936 was on the Arran via the Kyles run. She served as the minesweeper HMS *Goatfell* from 1939 onwards and was from 1941 an auxiliary anti-aircraft vessel on the Thames. Post-war, she served on various services from Gourock and Wemyss Bay until she took up the Ayr excursion service in 1954. She was converted to oil-firing in 1955. She closed the Ayr excursion service at the end of the 1964 season and from 1965 was based at Craigendoran as a successor to *Jeanie Deans*. She was on the afternoon cruise round Bute, but occasionally swapped rosters with *Waverley*. On two spells in 1969 she served on the Gourock–Tarbert service, from 14 to 23 April on charter to David MacBrayne Ltd, and from 1 to 8 October for the CSP. The latter was her final spell in service and she was sold in 1970 for use as a restaurant named Ole Caledonia, moored on the Thames in London near Waterloo Bridge. On 27 April 1980 she was ravaged by fire and was later scrapped at Grays, Essex. Her engines were rescued and are now on display at the Hollycombe Steam in the Country museum at Liphook, Hampshire, where they have occasionally been steamed using a portable boiler.

A further paddle steamer, *Marchioness of Lorne*, appeared in 1935. She was a smaller and slower version of the previous year's two steamers, and was placed on the Holy Loch service. She was not called up for war service and was moved to the Wemyss Bay–Largs, Millport and Kilchattan Bay service in summer 1953. There were a lot of complaints about her lack of speed. She was withdrawn at the end of that summer and was laid up in Greenock Albert Harbour. The year 1954 saw a final spell of service on the Millport run from 22 May until 8 June. She was sold for breaking up at Port Glasgow in 1955.

In 1935 a new small motor vessel, *Wee Cumbrae*, was built for a new service from Largs to Millport. This was to meet competition from the privately owned *Cramond Brig*. She was used as a tender at Rothesay during the war, and was on the Gourock–Dunoon service in 1947. In 1953 she was sold for use in Brunei.

In October 1935 Williamson-Buchanan Steamers Ltd was taken over by the CSP, along with the paddle steamers *Kylemore*, *Eagle III* and *Queen Empress* and the turbines *King Edward* and *Queen Mary II*. They operated on all-the-way services from Glasgow. A new company, Williamson-Buchanan Steamers (1936) Ltd, was formed to operate them.

Kylemore had been built in 1897 for Captain John Williamson, but he had sold her prior to completion for use on the Sussex coast, where she sailed as *Britannia*. In 1904 she had been sold to the GSWR, where she served as *Vulcan* until finally passing to Captain Williamson in 1908. She ran for him on a service from Rothesay to Glasgow, berthing overnight at the Bute capital. She was used for minesweeping from 1915 until 1919 and returned to her pre-war employment in 1920. She remained on her previous service after the CSP takeover with occasional sailings on the Wemyss Bay–Rothesay and Millport services. In December 1939 she was requisitioned by the Admiralty and converted to a minesweeper. She was sunk by bombing off Harwich on 21 August 1940.

King Edward had been built in 1901 as the world's first turbine-powered commercial steamer for the Turbine Steamer Syndicate (Captain John Williamson, William Denny shipbuilders and the Parsons Marine Steam Turbine Co.), which became Turbine Steamers Ltd in 1902. She ran from Fairlie to Campbeltown in her first season and to Inveraray from 1902. She was taken over by the Admiralty in February 1915 and served as a troopship in the English Channel and, in 1919, as an ambulance transport in the White Sea in support of the

White Russian Forces. In 1920 she returned to Clyde service, running from Greenock, Gourock, Wemyss Bay and Fairlie to Campbeltown. In 1927, with the advent of *King George V*, she was transferred to Williamson-Buchanan Steamers Ltd, under the same ownership, and moved to the 10.00 sailing from Glasgow to Rothesay and the Arran Coast. In 1933, when *Queen Mary* appeared, she moved to the 11.00 sailing to Tighnabruaich. During the Second World War she was used as a tender on the Clyde to troopships moored at the Tail of the Bank, and returned to the 11.00 Glasgow–Tighnabruaich sailing in 1946. She was withdrawn after the 1951 season and scrapped at Troon in the following summer. Her turbines were preserved by Glasgow Corporation in Kelvingrove Museum and were on display in the Scottish Maritime Museum in Irvine in the early years of the millennium; one is now in the Riverside Museum in Glasgow.

Eagle III had been built in 1910 for Buchanan Steamers Ltd. She had a single-cylinder diagonal engine, the last such built for a Clyde steamer. She had a promenade deck right to the bow and the sides of the main deck open underneath, like the CSP Duchesses of the 1890s. She was employed on the service from Glasgow to Rothesay, with an afternoon cruise from there. Initially she was very tender, with a considerable list with a crowd of passengers aboard, but this was corrected by a return visit to her builders, where the hull was remodelled below the waterline. She served from 1916 until 1919 as a minesweeper, based at Grimsby and Harwich. After the war she returned to her previous employment, being on the 11.00 sailing from Glasgow until 1932, and was then on the 09.30 sailing. In 1936 she ran from Glasgow to Lochgoilhead. Around the beginning of September 1939 she evacuated the patients of Gartnavel

mental hospital to Ardrishaig and in the following month was requisitioned and converted to the minesweeper HMS *Oriole*. She survived the war, but because of her antiquated engine and obsolete haystack boiler she was not reconditioned, and, after a period laid up in the Holy Loch, was sold for scrapping in Port Glasgow in August 1946.

Queen-Empress had been built in 1912 for John Williamson & Co. She had a full-length promenade deck, the sides of the main deck were plated in to the bow and she was fitted with two-cylinder compound diagonal machinery. She initially ran from Glasgow to Rothesay and to Lochgoilhead. In 1915 she was used as a troop transport from Southampton to various French ports, and was converted to a minesweeper in October of that year. In 1919 she went to the White Sea, where she was used as an ambulance transport in the campaign in support of the White Russian Forces. She returned to Clyde service in 1920, running long-distance excursions from the Clyde coast resorts, and was also on the Glasgow–Rothesay and Lochgoilhead services. From 1936 she was used on rail-connected services from Greenock, Gourock and Wemyss Bay. In March 1938 her funnel was painted CSP yellow with a black top. In October 1939 she was again converted to a minesweeper and served her country until the end of the conflict. She was not deemed worthy of reconditioning and was sold for scrapping in August 1946.

The turbine steamer *Queen Mary* had been built in 1933 for Williamson-Buchanan Steamers and was described as 'Britain's Finest Pleasure Steamer'. Her promenade deck contained a large observation saloon and her upper deck extended from below her bridge almost to the stern. She was placed on the 10.00 service from Glasgow to Rothesay, with an afternoon cruise, usually to the Arran Coast. In spring

1935 her name was changed to *Queen Mary II* following a request from Cunard-White Star Line for the use of the name *Queen Mary* on their new transatlantic liner. Her funnels were painted CSP yellow with a black top in December 1939, until then having been in the Williamson-Buchanan white with a black top. She remained on the Firth during the war years and was used on the Gourock–Dunoon service almost exclusively. In 1946 she reverted to the 10.00 sailing from Glasgow, and in 1952 to the 11.00 sailing to Tighnabruaich, following the demise of *King Edward*. In 1957 she was reboiled and a single large funnel replaced her previous two funnels. From 1965 she was used down Firth on Saturdays and in 1970 was based at Gourock, mainly on a Round Bute cruise. From 1971 she replaced *Duchess of Hamilton* on the Campbeltown sailings. In spring 1971 she had a major refit, with the dining saloon forwards being converted to a cafeteria. She continued in service under the Caledonian MacBrayne flag until the 1977 season, her original name having been restored in May 1976 and Glasgow sailings having been reintroduced from 1976, twice weekly from Anderston Quay, in response to revived sailings from the city by the preserved *Waverley*. She was laid up in the East India Harbour, Greenock, after the 1977 season and was sold firstly to Glasgow District Council for preservation as a floating museum, then in 1980 for conversion to a floating restaurant and again in 1981 for use as a floating restaurant in the Thames. She opened on the Thames Embankment in 1989 after further changes in ownership, with two very thin funnels replacing her single one and her turbines removed. These funnels had several rather garish paint jobs over the ensuing two decades. In 2009 she was sold for proposed use as a floating restaurant in La Rochelle, France, and was towed to Tilbury, where she remains. A further sale at auction in August 2011 has resulted in no progress. There are plans afoot to bring her back to the Clyde as a museum ship, but a lot of money would be needed for such a move. A group called the Friends of *Queen Mary* has been formed to look into everything possible to ensure a future is secured for her.

In 1936 a further, smaller, turbine was built for the CSP, *Marchioness of Graham*, designed for the Ardrossan–Arran service. She had a single funnel and no upper deck available for passengers. Her turbines were single reduction geared. She had small saloons fore and aft on the promenade deck. During the Second World War she remained on the Clyde, and operated from Fairlie to Millport and Brodick. In 1946 she was used for excursions, and from 1947 until 1953 was the Ayr excursion steamer, giving extra sailings on the Arran run at weekends. The years 1955 and 1956 saw her full-time on the Arran run and in 1957 she was used on excursion sailings from Largs. By now she was the last remaining coal-fired steamer in the CSP fleet, and was withdrawn at the end of the summer of 1957. In January 1959 she was sold to Greek owners under the name *Theo*, where she was dieselised and rebuilt from water level upwards. Changes of name followed to *Hellas*, *Nea Hellas*, *Galaxias* and *El Greco*. From 1963 cabin accommodation was added and she was used as a cruise ship; she was laid up in January 1968 after her owners filed for bankruptcy. She was finally scrapped in 1977.

In 1936 a new motor vessel appeared on Loch Awe, named *Countess of Breadalbane*, replacing the steamer of that name. She continued to run from Lochawe station to Ford until she was withdrawn after the 1951 season. In 1952 she was moved to Loch Fyne by road and was rebuilt for Clyde service. She operated a variety of feeder runs and short cruises and was, from 1965, on the Largs–Millport service, and from 1967 on the Holy Loch service until she was withdrawn in May 1971. In November 1971 she was sold on to Roy Ritchie and renamed *Countess of Kempock*, and in May 1972 she was was placed on a revived service from Gourock to Kilcreggan and Kilmun. In 1978 Mr Ritchie died and she was sold to Offshore Workboats Ltd, who chartered her to Staffa Marine for services from Ulva Ferry on Mull to Staffa and Iona for the 1979 and 1980 seasons, and at some time around then she operated from Oban to Tobermory. In 1982 she was sold to Maid of the Loch Ltd, partly owned by Ind Cope Alloa Brewery Co. Ltd, for use on Loch Lomond, replacing *Maid of the Loch*, and was renamed *Countess Fiona*. A dummy funnel was added to her, and two masts. In 1989 a full-width deck housing was added and a new funnel, but that was her final season and she was then laid up on the slipway at Balloch until broken up by a bulldozer some years later during preparatory work for the Lomond Shores development.

In 1936 a small engines-aft cargo motor vessel named *Arran Mail* came into service. She operated an early morning service from Ardrossan to Brodick with mails, newspapers and cargo. She spent the war years as a tender based at Gourock. She was replaced by the cargo steamer *Arran* in 1949 and operated some luggage runs from Fairlie to Millport in summer 1950. She was sold in December 1951, and again in September 1954, to owners in Gibraltar, for whom she was renamed *Saint Ernest*. Sold again to owners in Alderney, she was lost with all hands in January 1962 en route from Alderney to Newhaven with a cargo of vegetables and flowers.

In 1937, two new paddle steamers of the disguised paddle design were built for the CSP, *Jupiter* and *Juno*. Slightly shorter than the 1934 duo, they had two funnels and triple expansion engines. *Jupiter* entered service first. Space for cars was again provided between the funnels, and they entered service from Gourock and Wemyss Bay to Rothesay and the Kyles of Bute. Both were requisitioned by the Admiralty in September 1939 and converted to minesweepers, being renamed HMS *Scawfell* and HMS *Helvellyn* respectively. *Juno* was sunk by a bomb in Surrey Commercial Docks, London, on 19 March 1941. *Jupiter* returned to the Clyde in 1945 and was the first steamer that had seen war service to resume operations on the Clyde, on the Holy Loch service in February 1946. Her post-war service was similar to that prior to the conflict, from Gourock and Wemyss Bay to Rothesay. She was converted to oil-firing in the winter of 1956/57, and the summer of 1957 saw her on a Glasgow–Lochgoilhead service on Sunday afternoons. She was withdrawn from service after the 1957 season and was sold in May 1960 and resold for scrapping at Dublin in April 1961.

In 1938 two small motor vessels, *Ashton* and *Leven*, were built for a service from Glasgow (Bridge Wharf) to off Clydebank to enable visitors to the Empire Exhibition to view the shipyards and the new Cunarder, *Queen Elizabeth*, under construction. They repeated these sailings in 1939 and were used as tenders on the Clyde during the war years. In 1946 they opened an hourly Gourock–Dunoon service. In 1947 *Leven* swapped with *Wee Cumbrae* and went to the Largs–Millport service, where she was soon joined by *Ashton*. *Leven* spent a spell on a service from Gourock to Kilcreggan and Blairmore in January 1952. Both had passenger toilet accommodation added aft around this time. Both were withdrawn after the 1964 summer. Ashton was sold in 1965

to Roy Ritchie and renamed *Gourockian*, and again sold in 1971 to operate the Fleetwood–Knott End ferry, for which she was renamed *Wyre Lady*. In 1976 she was sold to run on the River Severn, and in 1977 to operate on the Sheffield & South Yorkshire Navigation, where she remains today. *Leven* was sold in 1965 to an owner at Larne, and soon after for use at Paignton, where she was renamed *Pride of the Bay*. In 1985 she was sold for use in Jersey, and in 1999 to an owner at Weston-super-Mare, where she was renamed *Bristol Queen* and ran to Steep Holm Island until 2010. At the time of writing she is reportedly undergoing a major refit with the aim of returning her to service.

In 1938 a new steam bucket dredger, *Carrick*, was built for service at Ayr. She was transferred to the Docks & Inland Waterways Executive in 1950 and was hulked in 1982.

The years of the Second World War saw some, but not all, of the CSP fleet called up to serve their country, and there was not the necessity of relying on chartered tonnage that there had been in the previous war. The demand for pleasure cruises evaporated, but the steamers were extremely busy with military personnel and were used to tender to the troopships moored at the Tail of the Bank.

Top: Glen Sannox in her 1924 colours arriving at Lamlash.

Bottom: Mercury in 1923, still with the grey hull, but with the 'tartan lum'.

Above left: Mercury at speed in the Firth in her post-1925 colours.

Above right: Glen Rosa in her 1925 condition.

Right: Jupiter arriving at Rothesay in her 1923 colours, still with the GSWR grey hull.

A stern view of *Jupiter* in CSP/LMS colours.

Juno departing Ayr in her 1924 colour scheme with the 'tartan lum'.

Juno and *Glen Sannox* berthed at Ayr in the late 1920s. The Arran service did not run on a Sunday, and on occasion *Glen Sannox* substituted for *Juno* on the Sunday cruises from Ayr.

The 325 hp compound diagonal engines of *Juno*.

The paddle tug *Troon* of 1902, which was based at Troon.

The former GSWR turbine steamer *Atalanta* off Lamlash in the 1924 colour scheme.

Atalanta in her post-1925 colours, entering Ardrossan harbour.

Glen Sannox at Brodick Pier with a large crowd of passengers on board.

Glen Sannox laid up in Albert Harbour, Greenock, in 1952 between her withdrawal from service and her sale for scrapping.

Duchess of Montrose in her original condition with a stump mainmast, prior to 1934.

Duchess of Montrose departs Campbeltown in July 1964, and is seen here from *Caledonia*, shortly to depart for Brodick and Ayr.

Duchess of Hamilton berthed at Campbeltown in August 1968.

Duchess of Hamilton at Arrochar on a Clyde River Steamer Club charter from Ayr on 7 September 1968.

A tinted postcard view of *Mercury*.

Before the car ferry: *Mercury* taking a car on board at Millport by means of two planks.

Caledonia, on trials off Gourock, on a Robertson of Gourock postcard view.

Caledonia arriving at Brodick in July 1968.

Caledonia arriving at Gourock in her final month in service, September 1969.

Old Caledonia as a pub on the Thames, 1979.

The remains of *Old Caledonia* after her destruction by fire on 27 April 1980.

The triple expansion engines from *Caledonia* on display at the Hollycombe Collection, Liphook, Hampshire in 1995.

Marchioness of Lorne off Gourock in 1952, showing the wheelhouse added in 1948.

Above: A well-filled *Kylemore* departing from Bridge Wharf on her afternoon sailing for Rothesay during the 1920s.

Left: The CSP's first motor vessel, *Wee Cumbrae*, arriving at Gourock.

Opposite page: King Edward in Rothesay Bay in an Edwardian postcard view, which has erroneously given her CSP funnel colours, colours she did not adopt until December 1939.

S. King Edward leaving Rothesay

King Edward arriving at Dunoon between 1937 and 1939, with *Juno* at the pier. Note *Marchioness of Lorne* in the background, heading south of Kirn.

Eagle III at Rothesay between 1937 and 1939, with *Jupiter* astern of her.

Above: Eagle III arriving at Dunoon.

Left: Queen-Empress at Girvan on one of her long day excursions, 1935.

Above left: Queen-Empress approaching Millport, 17 August 1939. By this time the CSP yellow funnel had replaced the Williamson-Buchanan white funnel.

Above right: Queen Mary II heads downriver past Anderston Quay prior to the installation of a wheelhouse in 1948.

Right: Queen Mary II after the installation of a wheelhouse in 1948 and a mainmast in 1953, and prior to her re-boilering in 1957.

Above: Queen Mary II off Millport (Keppel) Pier on 5 September 1970, on the Clyde River Steamer Club 'Three Steamers' day trip. This shows the black hull colours, reapplied in 1970.

Left: Queen Mary II about to depart Glasgow (Bridge Wharf) for Campbeltown, 4 September 1969.

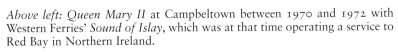

Above left: Queen Mary II at Campbeltown between 1970 and 1972 with Western Ferries' *Sound of Islay*, which was at that time operating a service to Red Bay in Northern Ireland.

Above right: Marchioness of Graham in pre-war days in a Valentine's postcard view.

Right: Marchioness of Graham arriving at Brodick in the mid-1950s.

Above left: Countess of Breadalbane at Loch Awe Pier prior to her transfer to the Clyde in 1953.

Above right: Countess of Breadalbane when on the Holy Loch service in 1969.

Left: Countess of Breadalbane carried a white hull from 1961 to 1964. The rust streaks seen here highlight the disadvantage of such a colour scheme.

Above left: Countess of Kempock, ex Countess of Breadalbane, in the Sound of Mull on an Oban–Tobermory excursion in 1981.

Above right: Countess Fiona, ex Countess of Breadalbane, as rebuilt in 1981, approaching Luss.

Right: Jupiter at Lochgoilhead on a summer Sunday in 1957, having sailed from Glasgow.

Above left: The short-lived *Juno*, which only saw three summers' service on the Firth.

Above right: The Arran mail and cargo vessel *Arran Mail* in the River Clyde off Erskine.

Left: Leven off Bridge Wharf in 1938 or 1939.

Above left: Leven arriving at Gourock, possibly when she was on the Dunoon service in 1946, or the Kilcreggan and Blairmore service in early 1952.

Above right: Ashton arriving at Millport from Largs in the early 1960s.

Right: Ashton as *Gourockian* between 1965 and 1970.

The dredger *Carrick*, built in 1938 for service at Ayr, seen there on 20 January 1959.

Chapter 4

THE BRITISH RAILWAYS ERA: 1948–68

On 1 January 1948 Britain's railways were nationalised and the CSP fleet came under the control of the Railway Executive (British Railways). The former LNER (London & North Eastern Railway) fleet was merged with the CSP along with the two railway steamers on Loch Lomond. From the LNER Clyde fleet came the paddle steamers *Lucy Ashton*, *Jeanie Deans* and *Waverley* and the paddle motor vessel *Talisman*, and on Loch Lomond the paddle steamers *Princess May* and *Prince Edward*. The Loch Lomond steamers had been jointly owned by the Dumbarton & Balloch Joint Committee (the North British and Caledonian railways until 1922, and then the LMS and LNER) from 1896 onwards, but were in practice operated by the NB and LNER.

Lucy Ashton was the veteran of the Clyde Steamer fleet, having been built in 1888 for the North British Steam Packet Ltd, the steamer-owning subsidiary of the North British Railway. New compound engines had been fitted in 1902, and were possibly the reason she had survived when all her contemporaries had long since succumbed to the scrappers' torch. She had originally operated from Craigendoran to the Holy Loch, but had spent most of her life on the route from Craigendoran to the

Gareloch. After the closure of Clynder, the last surviving pier on the Gareloch, in 1941, she had operated from Craigendoran to Greenock and Dunoon, and was the only LNER steamer not to be called up to serve her country in the Second World War. She made her last service run in February 1949 and was sold for scrapping in the same year. After her engine, saloons and paddle boxes had been removed, her hull was used by the British Shipbuilding Research Association for experiments with jet propulsion for a further year or so.

Jeanie Deans had been built in 1931 for the LNER. Her initial route was the Lochgoilhead and Arrochar service from Craigendoran, but from 1932 she was used on a variety of excursion sailings, including Round Ailsa Craig and to Ayr. She had the first three-crank triple expansion engines to be fitted in a Clyde steamer. An observation lounge had been added forwards on her promenade deck in 1932, and an aft deck shelter on her refit following her return from war service in 1946, during which she had served initially as a minesweeper and, from 1941, as an auxiliary anti-aircraft vessel based on the Thames. Post-war she operated from Craigendoran to Rothesay with, from 1953, an afternoon cruise round Bute from Mondays to

Fridays, and an afternoon cruise to Tighnabruaich on Saturdays. On Sundays, she either sailed round Bute and Cumbrae, or to Skipness, returning via the Kyles of Bute. From 1961 her sailings alternated weekly with those of *Waverley*. Ownership from 1948 had been by British Railways and was not transferred to the CSP until 1951. She was converted to oil-firing in the winter of 1956/57. Her final Clyde season was 1964, by which time she was indisputably the most loved Clyde steamer, being held in great affection both by enthusiasts and the general public. In 1965 she was sold to the Coastal Steam Packet Co. Ltd for use on the Thames under the name *Queen of the South*. She sailed from Tower Pier to Southend and Clacton or Herne Bay in 1966 and 1967 but was dogged by mechanical issues, and was withdrawn mid-season in 1967, being sold for scrapping at Boom in Belgium in December of that year.

Talisman was revolutionary when built in 1935, the first Clyde paddle 'steamer' not to have steam engines. She was on the Craigendoran–Rothesay and the Kyles of Bute service pre-war. Problems with her engine led to her being laid up in July 1939, but this was repaired by late May of the following year and she served as the anti-aircraft vessel HMS *Aristocrat* from June 1940 to February 1946, also serving as an HQ ship off Arromanches at the D-Day landings in June 1944, and escorting the first convoy up the River Schelde to Antwerp in November 1944. She had returned to the Craigendoran–Rothesay service in July 1946. She was on the Lochgoilhead and Arrochar service in 1952 and was laid up in 1953. After re-engining in spring 1964, she moved to the Wemyss Bay–Largs and Millport route, where she served until she was withdrawn in November 1966, being sold to Arnott Young for scrapping at Dalmuir in the following October.

Waverley had been built in 1947 as an indirect replacement for the 1899 *Waverley*, which had been sunk at Dunkirk in 1940. She was initially placed on the Lochgoilhead and Arrochar service but from 1952 this was reduced to thrice weekly, and a Round Bute cruise was substituted on the remaining three days. The year 1953 saw her on the Arran via the Kyles service once weekly and on railway connection services on Saturdays. From 1955 a cruise Round the Lochs and Firth of Clyde was introduced on a Wednesday and the Arrochar sailings were reduced to twice weekly. In the winter of 1956/57 she was converted to oil-firing and in 1957 a Friday upriver trip from Largs, Dunoon, etc. to Glasgow Bridge Wharf was introduced. From 1961 she swapped rosters weekly with *Jeanie Deans*. In 1965, following the withdrawal of *Jeanie Deans*, some round Bute cruises were added to her weekly repertoire, and in 1970, following the withdrawal of *Caledonia*, she was the last surviving Clyde paddle steamer. From 1971, following the closure of Craigendoran Pier, she was based at Gourock, but with a similar mix of excursion sailings. The year 1973 was her final one in service for CalMac, and on 8 August 1974, she was sold for £1 to the Paddle Steamer Preservation Society. They formed a company named Waverley Steam Navigation Co. Ltd to own and operate her. She re-entered service on 22 May 1975 with her funnels repainted in the LNER red with a black top and white band. Her preservation career is told elsewhere, but highlights have included her first sailings out of the Mersey in 1977, and her first visit to the south coast of England and the Thames in 1978 and to the Bristol Channel in 1979. In 1981 and 1982 she circumnavigated the British Isles; in 1982 she commenced offering a spring spell of sailings in the West Highlands; and in 1985 and 1986 she sailed from ports in the Republic of Ireland.

The winter of 1999/2000 saw a major Lottery-funded rebuild at the yard of George Prior in Great Yarmouth, returning her to her 1948 condition, with the exception of modern safety requirements, and the winter of 2002/3 saw a second stage of this, concentrating on the forward part of the steamer. She remains in service, running on the Clyde for most of July and August each year, with an autumn trip to the Solent and the Thames, a spring spell, normally about ten days, in the West Highlands and an annual trip to the Bristol Channel. Appeals have had to be made to the enthusiast fraternity from time to time to raise money to keep her operating and to get her through her annual survey and dry-docking.

The two Loch Lomond steamers surviving in 1948 were *Princess May* and *Prince Edward*.

Princess May had been built in 1898 and had two-cylinder simple diagonal machinery. She was withdrawn and broken up in 1953 on the arrival of *Maid of the Loch*.

Prince Edward had been built with compound machinery in 1910, although low water in the River Leven meant that she was stranded there for most of 1911 and did not enter service on the loch until 1 June 1912. She ran alongside *Maid of the Loch* for two seasons and was broken up at Baloch in spring 1955.

In 1949 Clyde & Campbeltown Shipping Co. was taken over by the Railway Executive, and its three cargo steamers, *Minard*, *Ardyne* and *Arran*, became part of the CSP fleet.

Minard had been built in 1925 for Clyde Cargo Steamers Ltd and was a typical engines-amidships small cargo steamer. She was on the Glasgow (Kingston Dock)–Rothesay cargo service, until this was withdrawn on 1 October 1954 following the advent of the car ferry service to Rothesay. She was then scrapped at Port Glasgow.

Ardyne was a sister of *Minard*, built in 1928. She was on a cargo service to Campbeltown until this was withdrawn on 31 October 1949. She was then used as a reserve steamer until she was sold in April 1955 to a Belfast purchaser, who did nothing with her. She was scrapped at Troon in autumn of that year.

Arran was built in 1933 to replace a steamer of the same name which had been wrecked on Barmore Island, Loch Fyne, in January 1933. She was an engines-aft steamer, like a larger version of a puffer, and was on the Ardrossan–Arran and Millport cargo service, replacing *Arran Mail*. In 1952 she was renamed *Kildonan* to enable the name *Arran* to be used on the new car ferry, and she was withdrawn in 1957 when the car ferry *Glen Sannox* entered service and was scrapped in the following year.

The years 1953–54 saw a fleet replacement programme take place on the Clyde and Loch Lomond, with the advent of the first car ferries.

The first of the new vessels was the paddle steamer *Maid of the Loch* on Loch Lomond. Built at A. & J. Inglis at Pointhouse, she was transported to Balloch in sections by rail and was re-erected on the slipway there, entering service on 25 May 1953 from Balloch to Ardlui. The pier at Ardlui closed in 1964, and calls there were replaced by a cruise to the head of the loch. Balmaha Pier closed in 1971, and Tarbert in 1975, leaving just Rowardennan and Inversnaid open, joined by the reopened Luss Pier in 1980. With the formation of the STG in 1969, ownership transferred from British Railways to bus operator W. Alexander (Midland) Ltd, although marketing continued to be done by the CSP. *Maid of the Loch* was under threat for many years because of poor financial returns and was finally withdrawn after the 1981 season. A string of new owners followed, with the steamer becoming increasingly derelict, until she was sold to Dumbarton District Council in 1992. Restoration efforts started in the following year and in 1996 she was sold to the Loch Lomond Steamship Co. Her accommodation has been restored and efforts are in place to obtain funding to return her to operation.

In 1953 four medium-size passenger sister vessels, the Maids of Ashton, Argyll, Skelmorlie and Cumbrae, entered service for the CSP.

Maid of Ashton was the first to enter service, on the Holy Loch service from Craigendoran and Gourock to Kilcreggan, Blairmore and Kilmun, with some calls at Hunters Quay, Kirn and Dunoon. From 1967 onwards she shared duties with the other three Maids. She was laid up in 1971 and sold in January 1973 for static use on the River Thames in Central London. Originally a private club, she has latterly been used as a restaurant. Her saloon windows have been extended to the bow. Initially named *Hispaniola II*, she later became *Hispaniola* and remains in use as an upmarket restaurant.

Maid of Argyll was mainly used on the service from Craigendoran and Gourock to Rothesay and was on the Arrochar service on Saturdays. From February to May 1970 she was on the Gourock–Tarbert Royal Mail service. She continued into the CalMac era in 1973, by that time running out of Wemyss Bay, including calls at the oil rig yard at Ardyne. On 1 March 1974 she was sold to Greek owners, who extended the landing platform to form an upper deck and renamed her *City of Piraeus*, running her on day cruises from Palaeon Phaleron marina to the Saronic Islands of Aegina, Poros and Hydra. She was superseded in 1976 by *City of Hydra*, formerly David MacBrayne's *Claymore*, and was then used as a relief vessel and on charters. In 1989 she was moved to Corfu, from where she ran day trips to Parga and Paxos, and in

1997 was ravaged by fire; she was not rebuilt after this, but left to rot and eventually scrapped.

Maid of Skelmorlie was mainly used on the Wemyss Bay–Largs–Millport–Rothesay route, including Cumbrae Circle cruises. A small mail room was added in 1969 to enable her to take on the Tarbert mail service, which she did from September 1969 to February 1970. She was sold in April 1973 to Italian owners for service in the Bay of Naples, and entered service in 1976 from Sorrento to Capri under the name *Ala*, having had some of her stern accommodation removed to convert her to a car ferry. From 1997 to 1999 she was chartered to Adriatica Lines for a winter service to the Tremiti Islands in the Adriatic, and in summer 2001 was chartered to Di Miao Lines for service from Pozzuoli to the island of Procida. She later operated from Naples to Sorrento until 2007 and remains in existence, laid up in Naples harbour and having recently been repainted.

Maid of Cumbrae operated various short-distance services on the Firth, including the then recently introduced 'Forenoon Café Cruises', the fare for which included a cup of coffee and a chocolate biscuit, normally a Gray Dunn's Blue Riband. She also operated afternoon cruises to such destinations as Dunagoil Bay, at the south end of Bute, and the Gareloch. In 1972 her aft saloon and galley were cut away to convert her to a stern-loading car ferry for the Gourock–Dunoon service, side ramps also being added. In April 1977 she was sold to Italian owners, renamed *Hanseatic* for her delivery voyage, and was in service for Navigazione Alto Adriatico from Trieste to Muggia under the name *Noce di Cocco* for a short while in 1979. She was then laid up at Trieste and was sold for use in the Bay of Naples as *Capri Express*. By 1983 she was on excursions from Capri with an inflatable swimming pool on the car deck. From 1984 she was on the Naples–Sorrento car ferry service and in autumn 2000 was running from Pozzuoli to Procida. She was sold for scrapping at Aliaga in Turkey in March 2006.

Arran, the first of the trio of side-loading car ferries, entered service on 4 January 1954 from Gourock to Dunoon. These ferries had a hoist aft of the passenger accommodation, with two manually operated turntables on it, and a U-shaped garage space on the main deck with another turntable at the forward end of that. Aft of the hoist were two kingposts with derricks, which were replaced by a single tripod mast around 1959. The original idea had been to load cargo aft but the increasing use of vans and trucks meant that there was little or no cargo to be loaded. A train delivered parcels, goods, etc., overnight, and they were stored until the first ferry in the morning on railway flat trailers, which were towed on board the vessel at Gourock, Wemyss Bay and Fairlie by motor buggies. Additional car spaces were created on the main and promenade decks aft of the hoists after the kingposts and derricks were removed. The passenger accommodation was basic, with a passenger lounge, a small cafeteria and a bar below the car deck.

Arran also served on the Wemyss Bay–Rothesay and Fairlie–Brodick services, alternating with her two sisters. A thrice-weekly service, mainly for cargo and commercial vehicles, also ran from Wemyss Bay to Millport after the withdrawal of the cargo vessel *Kildonan* in 1957. In November 1969 she was transferred to David MacBrayne Ltd for use on the West Loch Tarbert–Islay and Colonsay service. In early 1973 she was converted to stern-loading with the removal of the hoist and everything aft of where the hoist had been. She was used as a spare vessel after the advent of *Pioneer* in August 1974 and was withdrawn in 1979. In 1981 she was sold for static use on the River Liffey in Dublin as a

nightclub-cum-restaurant. She was built up over the former car deck. In 1983 this closed, and in December 1986 she was towed to Salford Quays for a similar use. She was broken up in 1993.

Cowal was the second of the trio of so-called ABC car ferries to enter service, in April 1954. In summer 1971 and 1972 she was on a new service from Fairlie to Tarbert via Brodick, replacing the Tarbert mail service, which was superseded by the new car ferry service from Lochranza to Claonaig in 1972. Latterly she served the oil rig construction yard at Ardyne, and was laid up in July 1977 when work there dried up. In May 1979 she was towed to Greece, and was laid up near Piraeus under the name *Med Star* until scrapped in 1984.

Bute, the third of the ABC trio, entered service from Wemyss Bay to Rothesay on 6 December 1954. In 1975 the horns on her lift were extended to enable her to berth at Armadale, and she served on the summer route from Mallaig to Armadale from then until 1978. She usually served as relief on Clyde routes in the winter months and also spent spells from time to time relieving *Loch Arkaig* on the Small Isles service from Mallaig. In June 1980 she sailed for Piraeus under the name *Med Sun* but no work was done on her there and she was scrapped in 1984–5. The reason these two never entered service in Greece was that the project leader died shortly after they arrived there, although *Med Star* was advertised to sail across the Adriatic from Otranto to Igoumenitsa around 1980.

In 1957 the car ferry *Glen Sannox* was built for the Arran service, sailing from Ardrossan in summer but berthing overnight at Fairlie, and with all sailings from Fairlie in winter. She was of similar design to the ABC ferries, with hoist loading aft of the passenger area and a large crane aft of the hoist which was rarely used. She was fitted with a bow rudder and a hydraulic lift, which proved to be very slow in actual operation. The passenger accommodation was a great improvement on the earlier trio. In 1964 she was the first member of the CSP Clyde fleet to receive a red lion on her funnel. In early 1970 a stern ramp was added. She was moved to the Wemyss Bay–Rothesay route on the advent of *Caledonia* for a couple of seasons, and from November 1971 was on the Gourock–Dunoon service. In the winter of 1971/2 the crane and all the superstructure aft of the hoist were removed. On replacement by *Jupiter* in March 1974, she moved to the Oban–Craignure service for one summer, and then spent two years on the Wemyss Bay–Ardyne service, serving the oil rig construction yard there. In the winter of 1976/7 she was re-engined at Hall Russell's yard in Aberdeen and her passenger accommodation was remodelled. She then went back to the Wemyss Bay–Rothesay service until *Saturn* entered service. In 1978 she took on *Queen Mary*'s role as Clyde cruise ship, with white lines round her hull and aircraft-style steps down to the car deck, which now had plastic chairs and tables with sun umbrellas on it. In 1978 and 1979 she did some sailings from Glasgow, but was not really suited to compete with *Waverley*. In 1981 the cruise programme was cut back to inter-resort sailings only, and in 1982 it was abandoned entirely until the advent of the cruises by *Keppel* in 1986. She was on the Oban–Craignure run in the winter months from the winter of 1977/8 onwards. In 1981 she spent a spell relieving *Columba* on her sailings from Oban to Coll and Tiree, to Colonsay and to Iona, for which purpose a ferry door was cut in one of her side ramps. She was used on a variety of services as a relief vessel during the 1980s and was sold to Greek owners in 1989. She was renamed *Nadia* and then *Knooz*, and a new aft superstructure was added. She operated in the Red Sea pilgrim trade, firstly as *Al Marwah*, and later as *Al Bismalah*, and was reported by some sources to have been scrapped in 2000. Around 2005, photographs appeared on the Internet of her aground and abandoned somewhere in the Red Sea and it is believed she is still lying there, rotting.

In 1965 the livery of the CSP fleet was changed in line with the new British Rail corporate image. All the ships received red lions rampant on their funnels, and hulls were painted in Monastral Blue, a colour which varies in photographs dependent on the weather conditions and cloud colours reflected off the surface of the water. Thankfully, the red funnels with the double arrow logo, which appeared on the remainder of the railway steamers, were not adopted on the Clyde.

In 1967 the Tilbury–Gravesend ferry *Rose*, built in 1961, was transferred north for the Largs–Millport service. After a week in service under the name *Rose* she was renamed *Keppel*. She introduced Voith-Schneider propulsion to the Clyde and had rather basic passenger accommodation, and a tall thin funnel-cum-mast; this was replaced by a larger one, which was wide enough for a lion, after a year or two. She sailed year-round until the winter of 1970/1. In June 1986 the Millport service was withdrawn and *Keppel* became the Clyde cruise vessel. Cruises were mainly in the nearer reaches of the Firth, with destinations including Carrick Castle and Tighnabruaich. She was noted for her lack of speed and was not really a success as a cruise vessel. She was withdrawn in 1993 and sold to a Greenock owner, who renamed her *Clyde Rose*, mainly using her on charters and special sailings, e.g. to the Millport illuminations. She was laid up after one season and was sold to owners in Malta in 1995; she regained the name *Keppel*, and still offers cruises there under the flag of Hornblower Cruises.

Above left: Lucy Ashton in 1948 in CSP colours.

Above right: Lucy Ashton at Craigendoran on 29 May 1948, with the bow of *Jeanie Deans* to the right and the funnel of *Talisman* visible to the left.

Right: The paddle box crest of *Lucy Ashton*, now on display at the National Railway Museum at York.

Above left: Jeanie Deans in her 1948–52 condition, with the wood-stained surround to the dining room windows.

Above right: Jeanie Deans at Arrochar in 1964, with passengers disembarking for the Three Lochs Tour.

Left: Jeanie Deans in the early 1960s.

Above: Talisman at Wemyss Bay Pier, with *Maid of Skelmorlie* lying across the end of the pier and a cargo liner outward bound.

Right: Talisman arriving at Largs in late summer 1963.

Above left: Talisman in Rothesay Bay in 1965 or 1966, with the lion on the funnel and the Monastral Blue hull.

Above right: Waverley heading up the Cowal coast in 1968.

Left: Waverley seen from the beach below Cloch Point around 1958, with the author as a young boy looking on.

Above left: *Waverley* at Brodick in 1970 or 1971, with an antiquated bus owned by Bannatyne Motors of Blackwaterfoot.

Above right: *Waverley* at Millport (Keppel Pier) on 4 September 1971, dressed overall for a Clyde River Steamer charter round Arran and Ailsa Craig.

Right: *Princess May* in 1948 with a CSP funnel, but still with a grey hull.

Above: Princess May in 1949, now with a black hull.

Left: Prince Edward at Balloch Pier in 1949–52 colours.

Above left: Prince Edward departing Ardlui with a white hull and yellow, black-topped funnel between August 1954 and the end of the 1955 season.

Above right: Clyde Cargo Steamers' *Arran* in CSP colours.

Right: Maid of the Loch being reassembled on the slipway at Balloch, 1952.

Above: Maid of the Loch in her present cosmetically restored condition.

Opposite top left: Maid of the Loch at Balloch in the mid-1960s.

Opposite bottom left: Maid of Ashton arrives at Blairmore on New Year's Day 1967.

Opposite right: Maid of the Loch on the slipway at Balloch in April 1981.

KEEP OFF PROPELLERS

Maid of Argyll arriving at Gourock in September 1970, with the stern of an ABC car ferry in the left foreground.

Above left: Maid of Ashton in her current condition as the restaurant ship *Hispaniola* on the Thames in central London.

Above right: Maid of Skelmorlie at Gourock during her spell on the Tarbert mail service, November 1968. Note the mail shelter added to the aft of the accommodation.

Right: Maid of Skelmorlie converted to the car ferry *Ala*, at Capri.

Above: Maid of Argyll on the Firth in an illustration from the 1972 summer timetable.

Left: Maid of Cumbrae departing from Largs, July 1968.

Above left: Maid of Cumbrae as converted to a car ferry, 1972.

Above right: Maid of Cumbrae, in her car ferry condition, departs Gourock in 1972.

Right: Maid of Cumbrae as *Capri Express* on a cruise from Capri, summer 1983.

Above left: The car deck of *Capri Express*, 1983, complete with an inflatable swimming pool.

Above right: Arran arriving at Rothesay in the late 1960s. Note the cars parked on the deck aft of the hoist.

Left: Arran in original condition, with goalpost masts and derricks aft, seen in a Valentine's postcard view.

Above left: Cowal at Dunoon Pier in September 1969.

Above right: Cowal and *Maid of Argyll* at Tarbert, 7 August 1970, *Cowal* having arrived from Fairlie and Brodick, and *Maid of Argyll* from Gourock, Dunoon, Rothesay and Tighnabruaich.

Right: Bute at Wemyss Bay in the Millport berth, between 1965 and 1969, with a Maid behind her and *Caledonia* across the end of the pier.

Above left: Bute departs Fairlie for Brodick on a winter service in early 1970.

Above right: Cars assembled on the hoist of an ABC car ferry. Note the manual turntables behind the three cars by the ramp and below the crew member with the white-topped hat.

Left: Bute at Dunoon, with Lochnevis arriving, in the 1965–69 era.

Glen Sannox arriving at Ardrossan in spring 1970, with a stern ramp, but still with the crane in place.

Glen Sannox in 1972, with the crane now removed.

Above: A deck view on *Glen Sannox* from the early 1960s.

Left: The lion on *Glen Sannox*'s funnel, the first in the CSP Clyde fleet, which was affixed there in 1964.

Above left: Former Tilbury–Gravesend ferry *Rose* at Millport in June 1967, prior to being renamed *Keppel*.

Above right: Keppel at Largs in summer 1967.

Right: Keppel en route from Millport to Largs in 1968 after a wider funnel/mast had been fitted.

Chapter 5

THE SCOTTISH TRANSPORT GROUP PERIOD: 1969–72

On 1 January 1969 the CSP was taken over by the Scottish Transport Group, which also included nationalised bus services in Scotland, and railway control of the company ceased after eighty years.

On 31 December 1969 the Swedish ferry *Stena Baltica* was purchased and became the first ferry in the fleet with bow and stern loading. She had been built in 1966 and had previously operated from Gothenburg to Frederikshavn and on 'The Londoner' service from Tilbury to Calais. She was renamed *Caledonia*, and, after she was altered to comply with UK fire safety requirements, entered service from Ardrossan to Brodick on 29 May 1970. Her vehicle deck was too small, her passenger accommodation was rather basic and a winter passenger certificate of 132 led to complaints from Arran residents. In 1974 she was transferred to the Oban–Craignure service in the summer months. She was withdrawn from service at the end of the 1987 season and was sold to an owner in Dundee for a proposed conversion to a floating restaurant, but no work was done on her and she was sold a year later for use in the Gulf of Naples, where she ran under the name *Heidi* from Pozzuoli to Ischia until 2004, when she was laid up at Naples. She sank at her moorings there on 10 July 2005 and was raised and sold for scrapping at Aliaga in Turkey.

The sidewall hovercraft HM2-011 entered service on 6 June 1970 and operated from Gourock to Dunoon, Rothesay, Largs and Millport, with cruises round Cumbrae and to Rothesay Bay. After two summers the experiment was not continued and she was sold back to the American parent company of her builders, Hovermarine in Southampton.

In winter and spring 1970, the MacBrayne car ferry *Clansman* of 1964 was used on the Gourock–Dunoon service, painted with a yellow CSP funnel with black top.

From 29 May 1970 the new MacBrayne ferry *Iona*, complete with CSP funnel without lions, replaced her on the Gourock–Dunoon service until November 1971. On 4 April 1972, after a couple of spells serving as relief on the Clyde routes from Ardrossan to Brodick and from Gourock to Dunoon, she was transferred to MacBrayne service in the West Highlands. She had originally been designed for a service from a new terminal at Redhouse, near the mouth of West Loch Tarbert, to Islay but the building of this terminal had been cancelled by Argyll County Council and her place on the Islay service had been taken by *Arran*, transferred from the Clyde, because she was too deep-draughted to sail on the narrow shallow channel to West Loch Tarbert Pier.

On 31 December 1969 the CSP took over the Bute Ferry Company Limited, which operated the car ferry service across the Kyles of Bute from Colintraive to Rhubodach with the ferries *Eilean Buidhe*, a water-jet-powered double-ended ferry dating from 1963; *Dhuirinish*, a former turntable ferry dating from 1956, which had been in service at Bonawe on Loch Etive until that service ceased in 1967 and had then been converted to bow-loading for the Colintraive service; and *Eilean Dhu*, a landing-craft-type ferry which had been built in 1940 and came to Colintraive in 1965. All three were sold: *Eilean Buidhe*, which had seen no service for the CSP, in late 1970 to Spearman of Kames, who sold her on for use as a yacht pontoon at Kerrera; *Dhuirinish*, which was spare ferry until the arrival of *Broadford* in June 1971, to a Mr Robert Beattie of Rothesay, who operated her on a new service from Port Bannatyne to Ardyne Point, reported to have operated for only two days. She was then sold to the Laird of Little Cumbrae, was noted on a barge near Oban in 1970, and ended her days serving Inchmarnock, where her remains still lie on the beach. *Eilean Dhu* saw little or no service for the CSP and was sold to Roy Ritchie of Gourock, who removed the engines and installed them in *Gourockian*, ex *Ashton*, and demolished the hull.

In May 1972 *Kilbrannan*, the first of what would become the eight-strong Island class of small bow-loading car ferries, inaugurated a new route from Lochranza to Claonaig, on the Kintyre peninsula. Although owned by David MacBrayne Ltd, she sported a CSP funnel, and her service was in the CSP timetable.

The recently purchased *Stena Baltica*, soon to be renamed *Caledonia*, in the Garvel dry dock in spring 1970.

Caledonia arriving at Ardrossan in her 1970–72 CSP colours.

Right: Caledonia at Brodick in 1972, showing the car marshalling area at that period, prior to the reclamation of land for the present area to the right of the pier.

Opposite page: Hovercraft HM2-011 departing from Millport.

Clansman at Dunoon on 7 February 1970.

Clansman arriving at Gourock in April 1970, with a CSP yellow funnel.

Above: Iona departing Dunoon with a CSP funnel in July 1970.

Opposite page: Iona off Ashton with a CSP funnel in summer 1970, with *Bute* or *Cowal* heading towards Dunoon.

Kilbrannan arriving at Claonaig in 1972 with a CSP yellow funnel.

Dhuirinish at Colintraive in a postcard view, with *Eilean Dhu* anchored off the slip, in use as a spare ferry.

Chapter 6

THE KYLE–KYLEAKIN FERRIES

On 1 January 1945 the LMS took over control of the Kyle of Lochalsh–Kyleakin ferry service with the vessels *Skye*, *Kyleakin*, *Moil* and *Cuillin*, and the CSP started advertising the service under their own name.

Skye was a wooden-hulled passenger launch built in 1922 and sold for private use in 1950.

Kyleakin was a two-car wooden-hulled turntable ferry built in 1928. She was sold in 1951 for use on the Glenelg–Kylerhea crossing, where she worked until around 1955. She was lost off Broadford in 1959.

Moil was similar, built in 1936 and sold in 1954 to the British Transport Commission, who used her as a workboat at Grangemouth Docks.

Cuillin was a two-car turntable ferry, built in 1942 and the first on the route with a steel hull. She was sold in 1954 to owners in Belfast, and in the following year to Newry Port and Harbour Trust.

In 1950 the timber-hulled passenger launch *Coruisk*, built in 1947, was purchased for the Kyle–Kyleakin crossing. She was sold locally in 1954 and was destroyed by fire in 1959.

The year 1951 saw the introduction of the two-car turntable ferry *Lochalsh* to the Kyle–Kyleakin crossing. She was renamed *Lochalsh II* in 1957 and was transferred to the British Waterways Board in 1958, for whom she served as a workboat on the Caledonian Canal until sold to owners at Nigg for work in connection with a fish farm and oil terminal there, where she was until around 1995.

The four-car turntable ferry *Portree* entered service in 1952 on the Kyle–Kyleakin service. She was renamed *Portree II* in 1965 before being sold to a Belfast owner who sold her on to the United Kingdom Atomic Energy Authority in 1967, for whom she operated from Orford to Orford Ness until 2004; since then she has worked as a barge and dive vessel based in Cornwall, and is still named *Portree II*.

A further four-car ferry was built for the Kyle–Kyleakin service in 1954. Named *Broadford*, she was renamed *Broadford II* in 1967 and was sold in that year, but the new owners did not take delivery. She was sold again in 1968 to Marine Transport Services Ltd of Cobh, Republic of Ireland, where she served until scrapped in 1981.

A six-car turntable ferry, *Lochalsh*, entered service on the Kyle–Kyleakin crossing in 1957. She was renamed *Lochalsh II* in September 1970 and transferred to David MacBrayne Ltd for the Scalpay service, being renamed *Scalpay* in December 1971. She served there until 1977, after which she was a relief ferry for CalMac's short crossings until sold in November 1979 to Ardmaleish Boatbuilding Co., whom she served as a barge until she was abandoned in the late 1990s.

In 1960 the last of the turntable ferries for the Kyle–Kyleakin service, *Kyleakin*, was built. She was a six-car ferry, a sister of *Lochalsh* of 1956. She was renamed *Kyleakin II* in 1970 on the arrival of a new *Kyleakin*, and was converted to bow loading in spring 1972 and renamed *Largs* in June of that year for the new Largs–Cumbrae Slip service. From the advent of *Isle of Cumbrae* in 1977 she became a spare vessel, and was used elsewhere in the CalMac network on occasion. She was sold to Ardmaleish shipyard at Rothesay in 1983 and laid up until sold to South Yemen in 1987, being taken there as deck cargo on a Dutch freighter.

The year 1965 saw the first side-loading ferry built for the Kyle–Kyleakin service, *Portree*. Originally she had side ramps and the wheelhouse was forward. With a capacity of nine cars, she went some way to alleviate the long queues of cars waiting for the ferry, with waiting times of three hours or more not being uncommon. In 1970 she was converted to bow-loading and was transferred to the Colintraive–Rhubodach service in May of that year, where she served until 1986. She was then sold to an owner at Sandbank to carry supplies to the US Navy ships in the Holy Loch.

In January 1967 *Broadford* appeared on the Kyle–Kyleakin service. She was a sister of *Portree* but had her wheelhouse aft from the beginning. Like her sister she was converted to bow-loading in 1971 and moved to the Colintraive–Rhubodach service in June of that year. She was sold in 1986 to the same purchaser in Sandbank then sold on to Welsh owners in 1988 and renamed *Boreford*. In the early years of the century she came back to the Clyde under the name of *Broadford Bay*, with her ramp removed, for use as a workboat, and was scrapped around 2005.

In July 1969 *Coruisk*, a sister of *Broadford*, entered service from Kyle to Kyleakin. In September 1971 she was converted to bow-loading and inaugurated the new route from Largs to Cumbrae Slip on 11 March 1972. She was sold in 1987 to an owner at Penzance.

Two new double-ended ferries, capable of carrying twenty-eight cars, were built for the Kyle–Kyleakin service in 1970, with *Kyleakin* entering service in June 1970 and *Lochalsh* being delayed at her builders and not entering service until 1971. Their large capacity led to the elimination of the long queues at each side. Both were sold in 1991 to Marine Transport Services of Cobh and were renamed *Carrigaloe* and *Glenbrook* respectively for use in Cork harbour on the crossing from Glenbrook to Carrigaloe, where they remain in service.

Kyleakin (1928) at Kyleakin. Note the chauffeur in the peaked cap by the driver's door of the car.

A rusty-looking *Lochalsh* (1951) at Millport, with *Maid of Argyll* berthed at the end of the pier in 1965–69 colours.

The 1965 *Portree* at the ramp outside the Lochalsh Hotel with the turntable ferry *Lochalsh* (1957) or *Kyleakin* (1960) at the near ramp in a postcard view.

The 1971 double-ended ferry *Lochalsh* off Kyle in a postcard view.

Chapter 7

CALEDONIAN STEAM PACKET (IRISH SERVICES) LTD

In January 1960 the dormant Clyde & Campbeltown Shipping Company Limited, some two years after its last ship, *Kildonan*, had been sold for breaking up, was renamed Caledonian Steam Packet Company (Irish Services) Ltd to operate the Stranraer–Larne service.

Princess Margaret of 1930 was chartered to the new company by British Railways Scottish Region, until she was sold in April 1962 for use under the name *Macau* from Hong Kong to Macau; she served there until she was wrecked in a typhoon on the night of 13/14 August 1971. She was salvaged and laid up until sold for scrapping in March 1974.

Until October 1961 the Dover–Dunkirk train ferry *Hampton Ferry* (1934) was used as a summer back-up car ferry on the route. *Princess Maud* (1934) was used as a winter relief for *Princess Margaret*.

The new car ferry *Caledonian Princess* entered service on the route in December 1961. She remained in service, operating from 1967 on various cross-Channel routes, until sold in 1984 for static uses as the nightclub *Tuxedo Princess*, initially on the Tyne and later at Glasgow. She was sold for breaking up in 2008.

From the spring of 1962 to 1965, the Dover–Dunkirk train ferry *Shepperton Ferry* (1935) operated on the Stranraer–Larne service while *Caledonian Princess* was away for overhaul.

The Holyhead cargo ship *Slieve Donard* was chartered in 1964 and the Swedish car carrier *Lohengrin* in 1965, both to carry cars only as a peak season back-up to *Caledonian Princess*. Neither carried passengers.

The Swedish car ferry *Stena Nordica* was chartered from January 1966 until 1971. She was the first car ferry on the route with bow and stern doors.

In spring 1966 and 1967, *Holyhead Ferry I* provided overhaul cover for *Caledonian Princess*, and, in the latter year, also *Stena Nordica*.

In March 1966, the lions were removed from the funnel of *Caledonian Princess*, and it was painted in the British Rail red, with the double-arrow symbol. In January 1967, the company name was changed to British Transport Ship Management (Scotland) Ltd, and so the brief spell of the CSP on the North Channel service came to a halt.

The 1931 *Princess Margaret* in a pre-war postcard view.

Hampton Ferry, seen here at Stranraer, offered a car ferry service in the summer months from the time after the loss of *Princess Victoria* in 1953 until the advent of *Caledonian Princess* in 1961.

Caledonian Princess at Stranraer prior to her adopting the red funnel with the BR double arrow logo in 1966. She had the lion on her yellow funnel from building in 1961, three years prior to any of the CSP Clyde fleet doing so.

The Holyhead–Dublin cargo roro *Slieve Donard* of 1959, which was used in 1964 to carry unaccompanied cars on the Stranraer–Larne service.

Chapter 8

FLEET LIST

Type	Name	Built	Entered Fleet	Disposed of	Builder	Engine Builder	Gross tons	Length	Engine type	NHP	Fate	Remarks
						Railway Steam Packet Company						
PS	*Royal Victoria*	1838	1841	1845	Barr & McNab, Paisley	Barr & McNab, Paisley	58	106.8 ft	Unknown	53	Scrapped *c.* 1875	Later operated on Mersey, Tay and Forth.
PS	*Isle of Bute*	1835	1841	1846	John Wood, Port Glasgow	Robert Napier, Camlachie	94	108.9 ft	Unknown	63	Broken up 1862	Wooden hull; later operated at Dublin.
PS	*Maid of Bute*	1835	1841	1847	John Wood, Port Glasgow	Robert Napier, Camlachie	91	110.5 ft	Unknown	70	Broken up by 1848	Wooden hull.
PS	*Pilot*	1844	1844	1847	Barr & McNab, Paisley	Barr & McNab, Paisley	192	137.4 ft	Steeple	60	Scrapped 1862	Later operated at Oban, on Loch Lomond and at Belfast.
PS	*Pioneer*	1844	1844	1847	Barr & McNab, Paisley	Barr & McNab, Paisley	196	159.8 ft	Steeple	95	Scrapped 1895	Later operated in the West Highlands.
PS	*Petrel*	1845	1845	1847	Barr & McNab, Paisley	Barr & McNab, Paisley	192	165.5 ft	Steeple	90	Scrapped 1885	Remained on the Clyde.
						Railway Steamboat Company						
PS	*Gourock*	1852	1852	1853	Scott & Co., Greenock	A. Campbell & Sons	75	113.7 ft	Unknown	50	Last record 1906	Renamed *Stella,* then *Phönix* and *Adler.* Sold for use at Memel and later Riga, Latvia.
PS	*Helensburgh*	1852	1852	November 1852	Laurence Hill & Co., Port Glasgow	Scott Sinclair & Co., Greenock	115	135 ft	Unknown	43	Wrecked 16 November 1859	Sold for use in Australia.
PS	*Dunoon*	1852	1852	November 1852	Laurence Hill & Co., Port Glasgow	Scott Sinclair & Co., Greenock	115	135 ft	Unknown	43	Lost in Bay of Biscay, 18 November 1852	Sold for use in Australia; lost on delivery voyage.
PS	*Glasgow Citizen*	1852	1852	1852	J. Barr, Kelvinhaugh	J. Barr, Kelvinhaugh	162	156.9 ft	Steeple	75	Lost between Australia and New Zealand, 14 October 1862	Chartered; sold for use in Australia 1854, sailed for New Zealand in connection with a gold rush, 1864.
PS	*Eva*	1853	1853	December 1853	Alex Denny, Dumbarton	Matthew Paul, Dumbarton	83	141.6 ft	Unknown	Unknown	Sank off Lambey island, 27 December 1853	Sold for use in Australia; lost on delivery voyage.
PS	*Flamingo*	1853	1853	December 1853	J. W. Hoby, Renfrew	J. W. Hoby, Renfrew	92	170.4 ft	Oscillating	60	Sank in mid-Atlantic, 22 December 1853	Renamed *Bell Bird.* Sold for use in Australia; lost on delivery voyage.
PS	*Lochlomond*	1845	1852	1854	Denny Bros, Dumbarton	Smith & Rodger, Govan	106	124.1 ft	Unknown	70	Broken up, 1864	Sold for use on the Mersey and at Preston.
						Wemyss Bay Steamboat Company						
PS	*Kyles*	1865	1865	1867	Caird & Co., Greenock	Caird & Co., Greenock	171	219.4 ft	Oscillating	120	Scrapped, 1889	Sold for use on the Thames and renamed *Albert Edward*.
PS	*Bute*	1865	1865	1867	Caird & Co., Greenock	Caird & Co., Greenock	171	219.4 ft	Oscillating 2-cylinder	120	Wrecked, 3 September 1878	Sold for use on the Thames and renamed *Princess Alice*.
PS	*Largs*	1865	1865	1869	T. Wingate & Co., Whiteinch	Caird & Co., Greenock	153	161.4 ft	oscillating	80	Scrapped, 1903	Sold in 1875 for use on the Shannon Estuary.

Type	Name	Built	Acquired	Builder (hull)	Engine builder	Tons	Length & engine	HP	Disposal	Notes
PS	*Victory*	1863	1865	1869 Barclay Curle, Whiteinch	J. Barr, Kelvinhaugh	126	176.7 ft Steeple	75	Sold in 1897 for use as a coal hulk at Newry	Remained on Clyde, renamed *Marquis of Lorne* in 1871 and *Cumbrae* in 1882. Remained on the Clyde, sold 1898 for use on the Tay and in 1904 to Spain, and renamed *Ares*.
PS	*Argyle*	1866	1866	1869 Barclay Curle, Whiteinch	J. Barr, Kelvinhaugh	141	177.3 ft Steeple	75	Scrapped, 1908	

Caledonian Steam Packet Co. Ltd

Type	Name	Built	Acquired	Builder (hull)	Engine builder	Tons	Length & engine	HP	Disposal	Notes
PS	*Meg Merrilies*	1883	1889	1902 Barclay Curle & Co., Whiteinch	Barclay Curle & Co., Whiteinch	244	210.3 ft diagonal, 2-cylinder Tandem Compound	205	Scrapped, 1921	Engines compounded, 1898. Sold to Brazil 1902, renamed *Maua*.
PS	*Madge Wildfire*	1886	December 1888	1913 S. McKnight & Co., Ayr	Hutson & Corbett, Kelvinhaugh	220	190 ft Diagonal Tandem Compound	95	Scrapped, 1946	Renamed *Isle of Skye*, sold for use on the Forth 1927, renamed *Fair Maid*.
PS	*Caledonia* (I)	1889	1889	1933 J. Reid & Co., Port Glasgow	Rankin & Blackmore, Greenock	244	200.4 ft Diagonal Compound	140	Scrapped, 1933	
PS	*Galatea*	1889	1889	1906 Caird & Co., Greenock	Caird & Co., Greenock	331	230.2 ft diagonal Tandem Compound	250	Scrapped, 1914	Sold for use at Genoa, Italy.
PS	*Marchioness of Breadalbane*	1890	1890	1935 J. Reid & Co., Port Glasgow	Rankin & Blackmore, Greenock	146	200.4 ft Diagonal Tandem Compound	140	Scrapped, 1937	Later used at Great Yarmouth and Newcastle.
PS	*Marchioness of Bute*	1890	1890	1914 J. Reid & Co., Port Glasgow	Rankin & Blackmore, Greenock	146	200.4 ft Diagonal Compound	140	Scrapped, 1923	Sold to the Admiralty, 1919.
PS	*Duchess of Hamilton* (I)	1890	1890	1915 W. Denny & Bros, Dumbarton	W. Denny & Bros, Dumbarton	553	250 ft Diagonal Tandem Triple Expansion	268	Sunk by a mine, 29 November 1915	Used as a minesweeper from 1915.
PS	*Marchioness of Lorne* (I)	1891	1891	1923 Russell & Co., Port Glasgow	Rankin & Blackmore, Greenock	295	200 ft Diagonal Compound	140	Scrapped, 1923	Used as a minesweeper 1916–20, did not sail again.
PS	*Duchess of Rothesay*	1895	1895	1946 J. & G. Thomson Ltd, Clydebank	J. & G. Thomson Ltd, Clydebank	338	225.6 ft diagonal	137	Scrapped, 1946	Used as a minesweeper 1915–19 and 1939–45; did not sail again.
PS	*Ivanhoe*	1880	1897	1911 D. & W. Henderson, Meadowside	J. & G. Thomson Ltd, Clydebank	282	225.3 ft Oscillating	123	Scrapped, 1919	Sold for use on the Clyde 1911–14, chartered back to the CSP 1916–18.
PS	*Duchess of Montrose* (I)	1900	1900	1917 John Brown & Co., Clydebank	John Brown & Co., Clydebank	321	210 ft Diagonal Tandem Triple Expansion	206	Sunk by a mine, 17 March 1917	Used as a minesweeper from 1915.
PS	*Duchess of Fife*	1903	1903	1953 Fairfield Shipbuilding & Engineering Ltd, Govan	Fairfield Shipbuilding & Engineering Ltd, Govan	336	213.3 ft Diagonal	199	Scrapped, 1953	Used as a minesweeper 1916–19 and 1939–46.
TrSS	*Duchess of Argyll*	1906	1906	1952 W. Denny & Bros, Dumbarton	W. Denny & Bros, Dumbarton	593	250 ft turbines, 3 direct drive	399 RHP	Scrapped, 1970	Sold for Admiralty experimental use at Portland.
SS	*Countess of Breadalbane* (I)	1882	1922	1936 Hanna & Donald, Paisley	Hawthorns & Co., Leith	95	99.9 ft Triple Expansion	30	Scrapped, 1936	
SS	*Lady of the Lake*	1882	1922	1929 Anderson & Lyall, Govan	D. Rowan & Sons, Anderston	68	92.5 ft Compound	21	Scrapped, 1929	
SS	*Sybilla*	1882	1922	1929 D. Fenton, Perth	D. Rowan & Sons, Anderston	37	61.2 ft Compound	11	Scrapped, 1929	
SS	*Carlotta*	1883	1922	1923 A. G. Gifford & Co., Leith	Ross & Duncan, Govan	23	56 ft Compound	10	Scrapped, 1923	
TSS	*Queen of the Lake*	1907	1922	1950 Ailsa Shipbuilding Co., Ayr	Ailsa Shipbuilding Co., Ayr	152	110.1 ft compound, 4-cylinder Compound	43 BHP	Scrapped, 1950	Laid up from 1939.
PS	*Glen Sannox* (I)	1892	1923	1925 J. & G. Thomson Ltd, Clydebank	J. & G. Thomson Ltd, Clydebank	610	260.5 ft diagonal	353	Scrapped, 1925	
TSD	*Kyle* *	1885	1923	1950 S. McKnight & Co., Ayr	S. McKnight & Co., Ayr	543	176 ft Steam Compound	90	Unknown	Bucket dredger.
PS	*Mercury*	1892	1923	1933 Napier, Shanked & Bell	D. Rowan & Sons, Anderston	378	220.5 ft diagonal Compound	248	Scrapped, 1933	
PS	*Glen Rosa*	1893	1923	1939 J. & G. Thomson Ltd, Clydebank	J. & G. Thomson Ltd, Clydebank	306	200 ft diagonal Compound	185	Scrapped, 1939	
PS	*Jupiter* (I)	1896	1923	1935 J. & G. Thomson Ltd, Clydebank	J. & G. Thomson Ltd, Clydebank	394	230.5 ft diagonal	273	Scrapped, 1935	

Type	Name	Built	CSP	Disposed	Hull builder	Engine builder	Tonnage	Engines	Power	Fate	Notes
PT	Ayr *	1897	1923	1930	J. P. Rennoldson, South Shields	J. P. Rennoldson, South Shields	124	2 cylinder 90 ft side lever	50	Unknown	Paddle tug; sold 1930.
PS	Juno (II)	1898	1923	1932	Clydebank Shipbuilding & Engineering Co., Clydebank	Clydebank Shipbuilding & Engineering Co., Clydebank	592	Compound 245 ft diagonal	325	Scrapped, 1932	
PT	Troon *	1902	1923	1930	J. P. Rennoldson, South Shields	J. P. Rennoldson, South Shields	130	2 cylinder 100 ft side lever	70 RHP	Scrapped, 1948	Paddle tug; sold 1930 for use at Middlesbrough, and in 1934 for use on the Mersey.
TrSS	Atalanta	1906	1923	1937	John Brown & Co., Clydebank	John Brown & Co., Clydebank	486	3 direct drive 210.4 ft turbines	200	Scrapped, 1945	Sold for use at Blackpool and Morecambe, used as a boom defence ship, 1940–45
TrSS	Glen Sannox (II)	1925	1925	1954	W. Denny & Bros, Dumbarton	W. Denny & Bros, Dumbarton	664	3 direct drive 249.9 ft turbines	382	Scrapped, 1954	
TrSS	Duchess of Montrose (II)	1930	1930	1965	W. Denny & Bros, Dumbarton	W. Denny & Bros, Dumbarton	806	3 direct drive 262 ft turbines	420	Scrapped, 1965	
PT	Walney *	1904	1930	1950	J. P. Rennoldson, South Shields	J. P. Rennoldson, South Shields	204	2 cylinder 120 ft side lever	66	Scrapped, 1952	Paddle tug; transferred to Docks & Inland Waterways Executive, 1950.
TrSS	Duchess of Hamilton (II)	1932	1932	1971	Harland & Wolff Ltd, Govan	Harland & Wolff Ltd, Belfast	792	3 direct drive 262 ft turbines		Scrapped, 1974	
PS	Mercury	1934	1934	1940	Fairfield Shipbuilding & Engineering Ltd, Govan	Fairfield Shipbuilding & Engineering Ltd, Govan	621	Triple Expansion 223.6 ft Diagonal	230	Sunk by a mine, 25 December 1940	
PS	Caledonia (II)	1934	1934	1970	W. Denny & Bros, Dumbarton	W. Denny & Bros, Dumbarton	624	Triple Expansion 223.6 ft Diagonal	193	Gutted by fire, 27 April 1980; hull later scrapped.	Used as a restaurant in London from 1971 to 1980; engines survive at the Hollycombe Steam in the Country Museum, Liphook, Hants.
PS	Marchioness of Lorne (II)	1935	1935	1955	Fairfield Shipbuilding & Engineering Ltd, Govan	Fairfield Shipbuilding & Engineering Ltd, Govan	449	Triple Expansion 199.5 ft Diagonal	140	Scrapped, 1955	
TSMV	Wee Cumbrae	1935	1935	1953	W. Denny & Bros, Dumbarton	Gleniffer Engines Ltd, Anniesland, Glasgow	37	2 4-cylinder 59.7 ft diesels	2 x 48	Unknown	Sold to Brunei owners, 1953.
PS	Kylemore	1897	1935	1940	Russell & Co., Port Glasgow	Rankin & Blackmore, Greenock	319	Compound 200.5 ft Diagonal	95 BHP	Sunk by bombing, 21 August 1940	
PS	Eagle III	1910	1935	1946	Napier & Miller Ltd, Old Kilpatrick	A. & J. Inglis Ltd, Pointhouse	432	Single 215 ft Diagonal	176	Scrapped, 1946	Not reconditioned after war service.
TrSS	King Edward	1901	1935	1952	W. Denny & Bros, Dumbarton	Parsons Marine Turbine Ltd, Newcastle upon Tyne	551	3 direct drive 250.5 ft turbines	399	Scrapped, 1952	
PS	Queen-Empress	1912	1935	1946	Murdoch & Murray, Port Glasgow	Rankin & Blackmore, Greenock	411	Compound 210 ft diagonal	178	Scrapped, 1946	Not reconditioned after war service.
TrSS	Queen Mary / Quinn Mary II / Queen Mary	1933	1935	1977	W. Denny & Bros, Dumbarton	W. Denny & Bros, Dumbarton	870	3 direct drive 252.5 ft turbines	350	Hull still in existence	Renamed 1935 and 1976; used as a restaurant in London from 1987 to 2009. Sold to Greece, renamed Theo, Hellas, Nea Hellas, Galaxias, Andros II and El Greco. Dieselised and rebuilt as a cruise ship.
TSS	Marchioness of Graham	1936	1936	1958	Fairfield Shipbuilding & Engineering Ltd, Govan	Fairfield Shipbuilding & Engineering Ltd, Govan	585	4 geared 220.2 ft turbines	267	Scrapped, 1977	
TSMV	Countess of Breadalbane (II)	1936	1936	1971	W. Denny & Bros, Dumbarton	Gleniffer Engines Ltd, Anniesland, Glasgow	106	4 12-cylinder 90.9 ft diesels	26 NHP 144 BHP	Broken up 1999	Moved from Loch Awe to the Clyde, 1952; re-engined 1956; later renamed Countess of Kempock, moved to Loch Lomond and renamed Countess Fiona 1982, withdrawn 1989 and laid up at Balloch.
TSMV	Arran Mail	1936	1936	1951	W. Denny & Bros, Dumbarton	Gleniffer Engines Ltd, Anniesland, Glasgow	137	4 12-cylinder 95.1 ft diesels	240 BHP	Lost at sea, January 1962	Various changes of ownership after she left CSP ownership.
PS	Jupiter (II)	1937	1936	1961	Fairfield Shipbuilding & Engineering Ltd, Govan	Fairfield Shipbuilding & Engineering Ltd, Govan	642	Triple Expansion 223.6 ft Diagonal	288	Scrapped, 1961	
PS	Juno (II)	1937	1936	1941	Fairfield Shipbuilding & Engineering Ltd, Govan	Fairfield Shipbuilding & Engineering Ltd, Govan	642	Triple Expansion 223.6 ft Diagonal	288	Sunk by a bomb in a London dock, 20 March 1941	

Type	Name	Built	Joined	Disposed	Builder	Engine builder	Tonnage	Dimensions / Engine	Power	Status	Notes
TSMV	Ashton	1938	1938	1965	W. Denny & Bros, Dumbarton	Gleniffer Engines Ltd, Anniesland, Glasgow	38	60 ft; 4 8-cylinder diesels	96 BHP	Still in service	Later became Gourockian at Gourock and Wyre Lady at Fleetwood and near Doncaster.
TSMV	Leven	1938	1938	1965	W. Denny & Bros, Dumbarton	Gleniffer Engines Ltd, Anniesland, Glasgow	38	60 ft; 4 8-cylinder diesels	96 BHP	Still in existence under refit	Later became Pride of the Bay at Torquay and Jersey and Bristol Queen at Weston-super-Mare.
TSD	Carrick *	1938	1938	1950	W. Simons & Co. Ltd, Renfrew	W. Simons & Co. Ltd, Renfrew	846	176.1 ft; 2 triple Expansion Compound	???	Hulked, 1983	Transferred to Docks & Inland Waterways Executive, 1950.
PS	Lucy Ashton	1888	1948	1949	T. B. Seath & Co., Rutherglen	A. & J. Inglis Ltd, Pointhouse 1907	224	190 ft diagonal; Triple Expansion	174	Hull scrapped, 1950	Hull used for jet engine tests, 1949–50.
PS	Jeanie Deans	1931	1948	1965	Fairfield Shipbuilding & Engineering Ltd, Govan	Fairfield Shipbuilding & Engineering Ltd, Govan	814	250.5 ft Diagonal	338	Scrapped, 1967	Sold for use on the Thames and renamed Queen of the South.
DEPV	Talisman	1935	1948	1967	A. & J. Inglis Ltd, Pointhouse	(1) English Electric Co. Ltd, Stafford (2) British Polar Engines Ltd	450	215 ft diesels; (1) 4 4-stroke 32-cylinder diesels (2) 4 8-cylinder diesels	312	Scrapped, 1967	Re-engined, 1954; both engines connected to electric drive for paddles.
PS	Waverley	1947	1948	1974	A. & J. Inglis Ltd, Pointhouse	Rankin & Blackmore, Greenock	693	239.6 ft Diagonal; Triple Expansion Single	2,100 BHP	Still in service	Sold for preservation, 1974.
PS	Princess May	1898	1948	1953	A. & J. Inglis Ltd, Pointhouse	A. & J. Inglis Ltd, Pointhouse	256	165.5 ft Diagonal Compound	130	Scrapped, 1953	
PS	Prince Edward	1911	1948	1955	A. & J. Inglis Ltd, Pointhouse	A. & J. Inglis Ltd, Pointhouse	304	175 ft Diagonal Compound	133	Scrapped, 1955	
SS	Minard	1925	1949	1955	Scott & Sons, Bowling	Aitchison Blair Ltd, Clydebank	241	143.1 ft Compound	53 RHP	Scrapped, 1955	
SS	Ardyne	1928	1949	1955	Scott & Sons, Bowling	Aitchison Blair Ltd, Clydebank	242	135.1 ft Compound	53 RHP	Scrapped, 1955	
SS	Arran (I) / Kildonan	1933	1949	1958	Ardrossan Dockyard Ltd, Ardrossan	Aitchison Blair Ltd, Clydebank	208	120.4 ft Compound		Scrapped, 1958	Renamed, 1952.
PS	Maid of the Loch	1953	1953	1981	A. & J. Inglis Ltd, Pointhouse	Rankin & Blackmore, Greenock	555	191 ft Diagonal Compound	1,060 IHP	Still in existence in a static role	Plans are afoot for a return to service.
TSMV	Maid of Ashton	1953	1953	1973	Yarrow & Co. Ltd, Scotstoun	British Polar Engines Ltd	508	161.3 ft diesels; 2 x 2 6-cylinder	650 BHP	Still in existence in a static role	Sold for static use in London on the Thames as a floating restaurant.
TSMV	Maid of Argyll	1953	1953	1974	A. & J. Inglis Ltd, Pointhouse	British Polar Engines Ltd	508	161.3 ft diesels; 2 x 2 6-cylinder	650 BHP	Damaged by fire, 1997, abandoned	Sold to Greece, renamed City of Piraeus, then City of Corfu.
TSMV	Maid of Skelmorlie	1953	1953	1973	A. & J. Inglis Ltd, Pointhouse	British Polar Engines Ltd	508	161.3 ft diesels; 2 x 2 6-cylinder	650 BHP	Still in existence but laid up	Sold for use in Italy, renamed Ala and converted to a car ferry.
TSMV	Maid of Cumbrae	1953	1953	1978	Ardrossan Dockyard Ltd, Ardrossan	British Polar Engines Ltd	508	161.3 ft diesels; 2 x 2 6-cylinder	650 BHP	Scrapped, 2006	Converted to a car ferry 1972; sold for use in Italy, renamed Noce di Cocco and Capri Express.
TSMV	Arran (II)	1953	1953	1980	W. Denny & Bros, Dumbarton	British Polar Engines Ltd	598	178.8 ft diesels; 2 x 2 6-cylinder	393	Scrapped, 1993	
TSMV	Cowal	1954	1954	1979	Ailsa Shipbuilding Co., Troon	British Polar Engines Ltd	598	178.8 ft diesels; 2 x 2 6-cylinder	393	Scrapped 1985/6	
TSMV	Bute (II)	1954	1954	1979	Ailsa Shipbuilding Co., Troon	British Polar Engines Ltd	598	178.8 ft diesels; 2 x 2 6-cylinder	393	Scrapped 1985/6	
TSMV	Glen Sannox (III)	1957	1957	1989	Ailsa Shipbuilding Co., Troon	(1) Sulzer, Winterthur (2) Wichmann Motorenfabrik	1,107	243.9 ft diesels; (1) & (2) 2 x 2 8-cylinder	2,400	Ran aground and abandoned in Red Sea, c. 2005.	Sold to Greek owners, 1989, renamed Nadia, Knooz, Al Marwah and Al Bismillah.
MV	Rose / Keppel	1961	1967	1993	White, Southampton	Lister Blackstone, Dursley	214			Still in operation	Sold, renamed Clyde Rose, sold to Malta, 1995, renamed Keppel.

Type	Name	Built	Acquired	Builder	Engine builder	Tonnage	Engine / Length	Power / Fate	Notes
TSMV	Stena Baltica / Caledonia (III)	1966	1969	1997 Norway / Langesunds Mek. Verksted, Norway	MAN Augsburg, Germany, 1964	1,157	2 9-cylinder 183 ft diesels	2,670 BHP Scrapped, 2005	Renamed, January 1970; sold to Naples owners, renamed *Heidi*.
Hovercraft	HM2-011	1970	1970	1972 Hovermarine Southampton	Cummins Diesels, USA	12	51 ft diesel	Unknown	Returned to the American parent company of her builders, 1972.
TJMV	Eilean Buidhe	1963	1969	1970 Dickie of Tarbert	Parsons Engineering, Southampton	34	2 6-cylinder 42.5 ft diesels	Unknown Unknown	Water jet-powered; beached at Colintraive 1971, when taken to Kerrera for use as a yacht pontoon.
TSMV	Eilean Dhu	1940	1969	1970 Unknown	Gleniffer Engines Ltd, Anniesland, Glasgow	28	2 4-cylinder 52 ft diesels	Unknown Broken up, 1970	Sold to Roy Ritchie, Gourock, and engines transferred to *Gourockian*, ex *Ashton*, 1970.
MV	Dhuirinish	1957	1969	1971 Fraserburgh / J. Noble (Fraserburgh) Ltd, Fraserburgh	Gleniffer Engines Ltd, Anniesland, Glasgow	29	50.6 ft diesel	Abandoned on shore of Inchmarnock	Originally operated from Taynuilt to Bonawe until 1966; sold to a Rothesay owner 1971, operated form Port Bannatyne to Ardyne for 2 days, sold on.
TSMV	Clansman	1964	1970	1970 Hall Russell Ltd, Aberdeen	Crossley Bros, Manchester	2,109	2 8-cylinder 220 ft diesels	2,400 BHP Abandoned off the coast of Sudan, 2002 or earlier.	Chartered from David MacBrayne Ltd, January to May 1970.
TSMV	Iona	1970	1970	1972 Ailsa Shipbuilding Co. Ltd, Troon	English Electric Diesels Ltd (Paxman Engine Division)	1,192	2 12-cylinder 230 ft diesels	1,600 BHP Ran aground on Cape Verde Islands, 2014	Chartered from David MacBrayne Ltd, 29 May 1970 to 4 April 1972. Sold 1997 to Orkney owners, renamed Pentalina B, used from Gills Bay to St Margaret's Hope, sold to Cape Verde Island owners Dec 2009
TSMV	Kilbrannan	1972	1972	1972 Glasgow / James Lamont & Co., Port Glasgow	English Electric Diesels Ltd (Kelvin), Glasgow	65	2 6-cylinder 63 ft diesels	300 BHP Still in service	Chartered from David MacBrayne Ltd; sold to Irish owners, 1992.

Kyle–Kyleakin ferries

Type	Name	Built	Acquired	Builder	Engine builder	Tonnage	Engine / Length	Power / Fate	Notes
MV	Skye	1922	1945	1950 Monance / J. Miller & Sons, St Monance	Kelvin	8	2 2-cylinder 33 ft paraffin	15 BHP Unknown	Sold, 1970, for use as a pleasure cruiser.
MV	Kyleakin (I)	1928	1945	1951 Goole / Webster & Bickerton Ltd, Goole	Kelvin	7	Unknown Petrol engine	36 BHP Lost at Broadford during a storm, 1959	Wooden hull; sold for use at Glenelg, 1951.
MV	Moil	1936	1945	1954 H. McLean & Sons, Renfrew	Gleniffer Engines Ltd, Anniesland, Glasgow	15	4 3-cylinder 41 ft diesels	36 BHP Unknown	Wooden hull; transferred to Grangemouth Docks, 1954, for use as a workboat.
MV	Cuillin	1942	1945	1954 W. Denny & Bros, Dumbarton	Gleniffer Engines Ltd, Anniesland, Glasgow	24	4 3-cylinder 44 ft diesels	36 BHP Unknown	Sold to Northern Ireland owners.
TSMV	Coruisk (I)	1947	1950	1954 Yorkshire Yacht Building Co., Bridlington	F. Perkins, Peterborough	19 46.1 ft	4 12-cylinder diesels	100 SHP Destroyed by fire, c. 1959	Wooden hull; sold to a Broadford owner.
TSMV	Lochalsh (I) / Lochalsh II (I)	1951	1951	1958 W. Denny & Bros, Dumbarton	Gleniffer Engines Ltd, Anniesland, Glasgow	24	4-cylinder 40.2 ft diesel	36 BHP Abandoned at Nigg, c. 1995.	Renamed, 1957; sold to British Waterways, 1958, for use on the Caledonian Canal, then to Nigg owners.
TSMV	Portree (I) / Portree II	1951	1951	1965 Dumbarton / W. Denny & Bros, Dumbarton	Gleniffer Engines Ltd, Anniesland, Glasgow	53	2 4-cylinder 66.5 ft diesels	160 BHP Still in existence	Sold to Ipswich owners, then to the United Kingdom Atomic Energy Authority and used as a ferry from Orford to Orford Ness; sold, 2004, for use as a dive barge in Cornwall.
TSMV	Broadford (I) / Broadford II	1954	1954	1967 Dumbarton / W. Denny & Bros, Dumbarton	Gleniffer Engines Ltd, Anniesland, Glasgow	57	2 4-cylinder 69.5 ft diesels	29 Scrapped, 1981	Renamed, 1967; sold to owners at Cobh, Ireland.
TSMV	Lochalsh (II) / Lochalsh II (II)	1957	1957	1971 Troon / Ailsa Shipbuilding Co., Troon	Gleniffer Engines Ltd, Anniesland, Glasgow	60	2 4-cylinder 82 ft diesels	36 BHP Abandoned, late 1980s	Sold to David MacBrayne, 1972, renamed *Scalpay* (II), then to Ardmaleish Boatbuilding Co., Rothesay, 1979.
TSMV	Kyleakin (II) / Kyleakin II / Largs	1960	1960	1987 Troon / Ailsa Shipbuilding Co., Troon	Gleniffer Engines Ltd, Anniesland, Glasgow	60	2 4-cylinder 82.5 ft diesels	36 BHP Unknown	Converted to bow loading, 1972; sold to South Yemen owners, 1987.
TSMV	Portree (II)	1965	1965	1988 Glasgow / James Lamont & Co., Port Glasgow	(1) Gleniffer Engines Ltd, Anniesland, Glasgow (2) Gardner Engines, Manchester	63	1) 2 4-cylinder diesels 2) 2 6-cylinder 75.8 ft diesels	36 BHP Thought to be still in existence	Converted to bow loading, 1970; sold to Sandbank owners, 1987, used as a workboat.

Type	Name	Built	Acquired	Disposed / Shipbuilder	Engine builder	Tonnage	Length	Engine	Power / Fate	Notes
TSMV	Broadford (II)	1966	1966	1986 James Lamont & Co., Port Glasgow	(1) Gleniffer Engines Ltd, Anniesland, Glasgow (2) Gardner Engines, Manchester	63	75.8 ft	1) 2 4-cylinder diesels 2) 2 6-cylinder 2 4-cylinder diesels	36 BHP Scrapped, c. 2005	Converted to Bow Loading 1970 Sold to Sandbank owners 1987, used as a workboat, renamed Broadford Bay
TSMV	Coruisk (II)	1969	1969	1986 Ailsa Shipbuilding Co., Troon	English Electric Diesels Ltd (Kelvin), Glasgow	60	80 ft	2 4-cylinder diesels	Unknown Unknown	Converted to bow loading, 1970; sold to Penzance owners, 1987.
TSMV	Kyleakin (III)	1970	1970	1991 Newport Shipbuilding & Engineering Co., Newport, Gwent	Gardner & Sons Ltd, Manchester	225	112 ft	2 8-cylinder diesels driving Voith Schneider units	Unknown Still in service	Sold 1991 to owners at Cobh, Ireland; renamed Carrigaloe.
TSMV	Lochalsh (III)	1970	1970	1991 Newport Shipbuilding & Engineering Co., Newport, Gwent	Gardner & Sons Ltd, Manchester	225	112 ft	2 8-cylinder diesels driving Voith Schneider units	Unknown Still in service	Sold 1991 to owners at Cobh, Ireland; renamed Glenbrook.

Caledonian Steam Packet (Irish Services) Ltd

Type	Name	Built	Acquired	Disposed / Shipbuilder	Engine builder	Tonnage	Length	Engine	Power / Fate	Notes
TSS	Princess Margaret	1931	1961	1962 W. Denny & Bros, Dumbarton	W. Denny & Bros, Dumbarton	2,552	314.2 ft	4 single reduction geared turbines	1,375 Scrapped, 1974	Sold to Hong Kong owners, renamed Macau.
TSS	Princess Maud	1934	1961	1961 W. Denny & Bros, Dumbarton	W. Denny & Bros, Dumbarton	2,883	319.2 ft	4 single reduction geared turbines	1,375 Scrapped, 1973	Overhaul relief 1961
TSS	Hampton Ferry	1934	1961	1962 Swan Hunter & Wigham Richardson Ltd, Wallsend	Parsons Marine Turbine Ltd, Wallsend	2,839	346.8 ft	4 single reduction geared turbines	Unknown Scrapped, 1973	Sold, 1969, for static use.
TSS	Caledonian Princess	1961	1961	1984 W. Denny & Bros, Dumbarton	W. Denny & Bros, Dumbarton	3,650	331.3 ft	2 double reduction geared turbines	3,650 Scrapped, 2008	Sold for use as a floating restaurant/nightclub at Newcastle, and Glasgow, renamed Tuxedo Princess.
TSS	Shepperton Ferry	1935	1962	1965 Swan Hunter & Wigham Richardson Ltd, Wallsend	Parsons Marine Turbine Ltd, Wallsend	2,839	346.8 ft	4 single reduction geared turbines	Unknown Scrapped, 1972	Overhaul relief 1962-1965
MV	Slieve Donard	1959	1964	1964 Ailsa Shipbuilding Co., Troon	British Polar Engines Ltd	1,593	292 ft	2 8-cylinder	3,000 BHP Scrapped, 1987	
MV	Lohengrin	1964	1965	1965 Fr Lürssen Weft, Bremen-Vegesack, Germany	Klöckner-Humboldt-Deutz	1,725	273 ft	8-cylinder diesel	1,900 Unknown	Chartered from Wallenius Bremen; sold to South African owners, 1979, converted to suction dredger.
TSS	Holyhead Ferry I	1965	1966	1967 Hawthorn Leslie (Shipbuilding) Ltd, Hebburn	Hawthorn Leslie (Engineering) Ltd, Hebburn	3,879	346.5 ft	2 double reduction geared turbines	12,000 SHP Scrapped, 1981	Overhaul relief 1966-1967
TSMV	Stena Nordica	1965	1966	1971 Ateliers & Chantiers de la Seine Maritime, Le Trait, France	Klöckner-Humboldt-Deutz	2,607	236.3 ft	2 12-cylinder diesels	600 BHP Burnt out and beached, 1980.	Chartered; sold to Venezuela, 1976.
TSMV	Antrim Princess	1967	1967	1986 Hawthorn Leslie (Shipbuilding) Ltd, Hebburn	At & Chant. de Nantes (Bretagne-Loire), France	3,670	346.5 ft	2 16-cylinder diesels	7,180 BHP Scrapped, 2007	Chartered to Isle of Man Steam Packet 1985–90 as Tynwald; sold to Italian owners, 1990, renamed Lauro Express and Giuseppe D'Abundo in 2003.

ACKNOWLEDGEMENTS

The photographs, etc., are from the author's collection, apart from a couple which are from the Iain Quinn collection. Many were originally produced for sale by the Clyde River Steamer Club, whom we thank most heartily. The drawings of the early steamers are from the Langmuir Collection and the Wotherspoon collection in the Mitchell Library, Glasgow. Thanks are also due to Iain Quinn for help in checking information, etc. Most of the basic facts about the vessels are from *Clyde River & Other Steamers*, by C. L. D. Duckworth and G. E. Langmuir, 4th edition, 1990: Brown, Son & Ferguson, Glasgow, and from the Ships of CalMac website and various Clyde River Steamer Club publications.

Want to know more about the Caledonian Steam Packet and its ships?

Join the Clyde River Steamer Club

Members receive two publications each year: the Magazine, which has historical articles about Clyde steamers and motor vessels, and the Review, which is a review of all passenger shipping services in Scotland in the previous year.

Meetings are held monthly in Jury's Inn, Jamaica Street, Glasgow, from October to April with a wide selection of speakers, both from the enthusiast fraternity and from the industry. A wide selection of photographs and club publications are available to purchase at these meetings.

Special cruise and coach-and-cruise excursions are organised from time to time.

Membership is £20 per year, with an introductory offer of £10. Contact Stuart Craig, Membership Secretary, 20 Earlspark Avenue, Glasgow, G43 2HW, or go to the website at www.crsc.org.uk.